America Eats

THE IOWA
SZATHMÁRY
CULINARY ARTS SERIES

Edited by David E. Schoonover

Nelson Algren

AMERICA

E·A·T·S

Preface by Louis I. Szathmáry II   *Foreword by David E. Schoonover*

University of Iowa Press ψ Iowa City

University of Iowa Press, Iowa City 52242

Preface, foreword, and tested recipes

copyright © 1992 by the University of

Iowa Press

All rights reserved

Printed in the United States of America

Design by Richard Hendel

Unless otherwise noted, all photographs
are from the State Historical Society
of Iowa, Iowa City. Place-names in the
captions refer to Iowa locations.

Library of Congress

Cataloging-in-Publication Data

Algren, Nelson, 1909–1981.

America eats/by Nelson Algren;

preface by Louis I. Szathmáry II; edited by

David E. Schoonover.—1st ed.

p.   cm. — (The Iowa Szathmáry culinary

arts series)

ISBN 0-87745-361-6 (cloth: acid-free paper)

1. Cookery, American—Midwestern style.

2. Cookery—Middle West.

3. Middle West—Social life and customs.

I. Schoonover, David E.

II. Title.   III. Series.

TX715.2.M53A44   1992   91-41109

641.5977—dc20   CIP

96 95 94 93 92 C 10 9 8 7 6 5 4 3 2

96 95 94 93 92 P 10 9 8 7 6 5 4 3 2 1

Contents

Nelson Algren in Chicago, near his apartment at 1958 W. Evergreen Street.
Courtesy of Louis Szathmáry.

Preface

LOUIS I. SZATHMÁRY II

In my native Hungary I was raised in a bookish family. From my great-grandfather on my father's side, my forebears were all book collectors, and when I had to leave just hours before the Soviet army arrived in the Transylvanian city where I resided and worked in the fall of 1944, I already had inherited and amassed a sizable number of books, mainly on Hungarian literature and other Hungarian subjects.

Arriving virtually penniless in New York in 1951 with only fourteen books in my small wooden trunk, I quite naturally continued collecting whatever books I could get hold of relating to anything Hungarian. At the same time, it became evident that my growing career interest in the culinary arts and food management would also lead me to collect books in these fields.

My first purchase was a book by Ludwig Bemelmans at the Marboro outlet store at 42nd Street and Broadway, where in 1952 all the remainder books were sold for nineteen cents each. Through the years, my Hungarian collection grew to some 22,000 volumes, of which about 12,000 have been donated to the Joseph Regenstein Library at the University of Chicago. Another 10,000 were donated to Indiana University in Bloomington.

My 22,000-volume cookbook collection has been at the University of Iowa Library in Iowa City since 1989. The rest of my culinary collection—including duplicate copies of the cookbooks at Iowa, archival documents, and objects relating to food, drink, travel, and tourism—

consists of some 200,000 items recently donated to Johnson & Wales University in Providence, Rhode Island.

But it is the cookbooks at the University of Iowa that probably have the widest appeal. Their significance goes far beyond being one of the largest collections of recipes from the fifteenth century to the present. They have proved to be a valuable source of information for many other disciplines beyond food and medicine. Yes, after Gutenberg developed printing, many of the early cookbooks were written by authors of medical books.

Cookbooks have been and continue to be helpful to researchers in history, science, economics, sociology, geography, and in related fields such as immigration and demographics. During the twenty-five years I nurtured and housed this growing library before it "graduated" to Iowa, it was busy with students working on doctoral dissertations, authors researching their books, and lawyers seeking facts and figures for cases.

American, English, French, German, Italian, and Hungarian books comprise the bulk of the collection, but the interested researcher or curious reader will find rarities such as the first cookbook printed in Czech and recipes in Polish, Russian, Serbian, Slovak, Spanish, Portuguese, and Scandinavian languages.

The books were printed in practically every state, many countries, and every continent. There's even a cookbook from Antarctica.

Many of the books are physically attractive, designed and produced by noted artists. Some of the volumes are huge; others are quite small. Some are printed on fine parchment, defying the ravages of time and clime, while others printed on more perishable paper remain healthy under the professional care provided by the library staff at the University of Iowa.

NELSON ALGREN AND *AMERICA EATS*

Shortly after our family—my wife, Sada, sister-in-law, brother, and myself—opened our little storefront Bakery Restaurant on Chicago's near north side nearly thirty years ago, Nelson Algren and some of his friends and hangers-on became frequent customers. For several years after opening we didn't serve alcoholic beverages. So his moochers stopped showing up, but Nelson kept coming. Apparently he liked the place. Although he was certainly not someone who got chummy-chummy readily, we easily became acquaintances and then friends.

Nelson often invited my wife and me to his table to talk. He also introduced us to some of his real friends, like Stephen Deutch, the photographer, with whom he lived in friendship during their Paris years, a friendship that continued after both settled in Chicago.

In a few years my wife and I were inviting Nelson to our home, where he could be a charming, almost bubbling conversationalist. But occasionally he would sit in a corner for hours without saying a word, then stand up and walk out with a grunted good-bye.

When H. E. F. Donohue's *Conversations with Nelson Algren* was published in 1964, we introduced the book to the Chicago news media at a Parisian Christmas lunch at the Bakery Restaurant. When Nelson had autographing sessions at other locations, Sada and I were always invited.

Some years later we learned, not from Nelson himself but from an item in a gossip column, about the auction he was planning at his apartment on Evergreen Street. Coincidentally, a couple of days later I ran into him on the street and asked about the auction. We were very welcome, he said, to come, browse, and buy anything we liked.

Even if blindfolded and handcuffed, I would have been able to recognize Nelson's home by its smell. It was an odor typical of a bachelor's apartment inhabited by one who stored huge amounts of magazines and papers for a long time, who chain-smoked with other chain-smokers

Caricature of Nelson Algren by Louis Szathmáry.

---

over the poker table set up in the kitchen, who kept his clothing clean but never threw anything out. The undertone of beer, bourbon, and wine was mixed in with the cold, stale smoke. The kitchen faucet dripped, perhaps for years, into some foil pie dishes piled in the sink. Yes, the odor of the dripping water was also a part of the general aroma, as were the shaving cream and soap smells from the bathroom.

As we entered the apartment, to the right, at the poker table, Nelson was talking to a few people, mostly curiosity-seekers; to the left, in one of the rooms, a young man from the book department of Marshall Field's stood behind a table covered with a sheet of paper on which a few items were laid out, designated for a silent auction.

That is when I first saw the typescript of *America Eats*. I had no chance to read it, but I looked into it and decided I must have it for my collection. To be sure, I bid higher than I felt I should. After we picked up a few magazines with Nelson's short stories and articles in them and he had signed all our treasures, the young man from Marshall Field's showed him the listing of bids. Nelson said, "Lou, are you crazy? You are bidding much too much for that manuscript. The recipes in it are lousy. It was a government writers' project. I did it because I needed the money."

I mumbled that I would like to collaborate with him to rework the recipes, perhaps publish them. He said that up to then he thought I was just crazy, but now he was sure I was sheer mad. But, he said, he needed the money and he appreciated my bid. A few days later I learned I was the highest bidder and the owner of the typescript.

All this happened shortly before Algren left Chicago. I believe I talked to him only a couple of times after I had the manuscript and only once—perhaps for fifteen minutes—about the recipes. I told him that I thought some of them were easy to follow, others sketchy, and a few impossible: for instance, the Flemish booya—60 gallons, with 30 pounds of ox tails, 10 pounds of beef soup bones, 4 fat hens, and half a bushel of tomatoes.

He laughed. He said the book was his but the recipes were not. He had collected them from various sources—housewives, farmers, sailors, tavern owners, greasy-spoon cooks—and wrote them down as best he could. He wished me luck in case I really wanted to do something with them.

Soon after, Algren left Chicago. The next time I thought about his manuscript in my library was when I heard the news that he had died. Stephen Deutch phoned to tell me there would be a eulogy in his memory at Second City and asked me to come and say a few words. I thought the best I could do would be to rewrite the Hungarian goulash and spaetzle recipe from Nelson's manuscript, make it into a tasty, authentic dish, and pass around a copy of the original typescript page along with the revised version that was to be prepared for the event.

That was for many years the only recipe I changed. When I was notified that the University of Iowa Press was planning to publish this work, I volunteered to prepare each recipe from the manuscript and then bring it into a form to make the upcoming book enjoyable reading and the book's recipes enjoyable eating.

The manuscript is from the early 1930s, so the recipes are from some sixty years ago. I felt that I alone could not undertake the task of preparing every dish according to the original recipe, then making the changes believed necessary, then rewriting the recipes and again preparing each one. I was fortunate to secure the understanding and cooperation of John A. Yena, president of Johnson & Wales University in Providence, Rhode Island, known to be the largest educational institution in the field of hospitality, food management, and culinary arts. Dr. Yena arranged for the dean of culinary administration, Tom Wright, and the curator of the university's Culinary Archives and Museum, Barbara Kuck, to assist me and for two teaching assistants, Steve Kilroy and Michael D. Pursell, to cook every recipe as many times as needed until we produced not only passable but enjoyable results.

Easy to say but not to do. For instance, none of us had ever tasted Portuguese, Welsh, Danish, or Norwegian ethnic dishes from more than half a century ago. So we really had no standards for our tests. But at the university, with several thousand students from more than sixty countries, we found those who could assist us with advice and guidance and could approve or turn down our results.

My main goal was to keep as close as possible to the original recipes. Yet, when you compare the recipes in Algren's manuscript and the revised recipes, you will find some significant differences.

What I realized—after forty years spent in the kitchen in the United States cooking, authoring five cookbooks, editing two reprint series, and writing a food column in the *Chicago Daily News* and then in the

Sun-Times every week for twelve years—is that the recipes submitted by the best cooks may be the most difficult to follow. Such cooks tend to assume that the readers know as much as they do and may not be sufficiently detailed in their instructions.

We noticed this, for example, with the Portuguese walnut pudding. Those not very well versed could indeed make a sad mess following the original method. But, after our changes in the instructions, not only my assistants but young friends with whom I shared the recipe could produce a wonderful dish.

What can happen to timing is evident in the Polish recipe for stuffed roast suckling pig. A suckling pig roasted "for one or two hours" would be a sad surprise because, even after 120 minutes and even if placed in a preheated oven, the meat wouldn't rise to 100 degrees in the thickest part of the hind leg. The correct cooking time should be at least two times or more for the suckling pig. On the other hand, if baked for three hours the Arabian mutton stew with prunes would be inedible.

I must admit that, as often as I tried the Danish beer bread, I didn't grow fond of it. I don't think I would ever serve it unless I had Danish guests who requested it.

Nelson separated some recipes from one another thoughout his manuscript even if logically they belonged together, like the polenta and its sauce. So I took the liberty of separating the Hungarian goulash from the spaetzle, for several reasons. First, the recipe itself is not what Hungarians in Hungary call goulash. We call this dish *pörkölt*. And, although once in a while we do eat it with the tiny egg dumplings, misnamed from the German cooking vocabulary as spaetzle, it is often served with boiled or baked potatoes, egg barley, or simply with crusty bread, salt sticks, or kaiser rolls. On the other hand, the spaetzle, or *galuska* in Hungarian, recipe in itself is a very good one and could be served with several other dishes from the book. It could be served with grated cheese and some melted butter as a pasta course right after an antipasto, before a main course; or it could be a side dish to several of the meat dishes.

I found that, except for the African vegetable dish with the eggs baked in the individual casseroles, there isn't one vegetable dish among the group or not even one that is predominantly vegetable. Many of the items have several meats in one dish, such as suckling pig and goose liver, ox tail and fat hens, pork and beef, or beef, pork, and chicken. And in most dishes, if any vegetables are included, they are mainly for color or flavoring—onions, garlic, celery, carrots, and tomatoes.

This brings up my old theory or pet peeve—something I talked to Nelson about years before I knew that he had written a cookbook. It is that all immigrants from all parts of the world arriving in the United States start to replace their everyday national dishes with their homeland's special holiday and festival dishes and Sunday meals. Germans in America don't eat daily German food, rather German Sunday fare. Similarly, the French, Serbians, Polish, Spanish, and others in our country favor their special-occasion meals. For this reason, I think it is natural that sixty years ago, when the United States was an active "melting pot," a young American writer exploring the traditional national dishes of his fellow Americans of Dutch, Russian, Italian, Mexican, and other origins overwhelmingly received recipes for national holiday feast dishes.

My two main drives in this research and development were to pay homage to Nelson Algren and to show my concern for our readers. I don't want readers to spend money and time on food that may not be enjoyed.

A final word of caution. We didn't try to duplicate the wine recipe. We did the testing during a time of the year when the grapes were not available, and we didn't have the time to wait for the transformation of the grape juices into wine.

Enjoy!

Foreword

DAVID E. SCHOONOVER

Nelson Algren's *America Eats* presents for the first time a gathering of peoples, regions, states, foods, stories, songs, and recipes harvested after more than fifty years. Algren collected the information for *America Eats* in the late 1930s as part of his duties with the Illinois Writers' Project, a branch of the federal WPA (Works Progress Administration, succeeded by the Work Projects Administration in 1939). He had joined the Chicago-based project in 1936, in company with such colleagues as Saul Bellow, Richard Wright, Margaret Alexander, and Arna Bontemps. The WPA interviewers, writers, and editors were responsible for creating a series of state and local guides with information on history, settlement, commerce, art, and architecture, as well as for gathering information on immigration, social and ethnic studies, and folklore.

Nelson Algren knew the ingredients in the midwestern and national cauldrons: born in 1909 in Detroit to parents of German-Jewish-Swedish background, he spent most of his early years in Chicago until the depression sent him traveling to New Orleans and southwest Texas. There brief jobs as a fruit picker, door-to-door salesman, carnival worker, and gas station operator gave him experiences and scenes that would be used in his first novel, *Somebody in Boots* (1935), "Dedicated to Those Innumerable Thousands: The Homeless Boys of America."

In 1937 Algren became the supervisor for the Illinois project, and he discovered that his interviewing and writing were closely allied with his interests in the lives of workers in Chicago's steel mills, packinghouses, and auto plants. He used much of this time to gather material on life in the Polish ghetto for his next novel, *Never Come Morning*, which was published in 1942 after he had finished with the WPA.

The "America Eats" staff was expected to produce a series of guides covering several regions of the United States. As pioneers in tracing American gastronomy, they would be describing types of immigration, settlement, and customs as these factors relate to food among members of national or occupational groups, communities, or regions. With Chicago as his primary base of operations, Algren concentrated his attention on the Midwest, ranging from Indiana to Nebraska and from Minnesota to Kansas. Although he completed his task, the work remained unpublished until now. By the early 1940s Algren and members of other "America Eats" projects saw their reports being filed away as the government turned its attention first toward national defense and then to war mobilization.

During the war Algren served with the United States Army Field Artillery and Medical Corps, with tours of duty in Wales, Germany, and France. He was honorably discharged in 1945. After the war Algren continued with his writing, winning the first National Book Award for *The Man with the Golden Arm* (1949); he substantially rewrote *Somebody in Boots* to become *A Walk on the Wild Side* (1956). In addition to novels, Algren wrote short stories, essays, travel books, poetry, book reviews, and the prose poem *Chicago: City on the Make*, but these works never achieved great popularity or received extensive critical attention during his lifetime. He was elected to membership in the American Academy and Institute of Arts and Letters only three months before his death in May 1981.

Algren's personal copy of the *America Eats* typescript, headed "Am Eats Algren" in pencil in his handwriting, had remained in his possession until March 1975, when he held a silent auction of his apartment's contents—appliances, furniture, manuscripts, photographs—before leaving Chicago. The typescript passed directly to his friend Chef Louis Szathmáry, who had immediately recognized the culinary, historical, and literary value of "Am Eats," as he explains in his preface to this volume. In 1987 Chef Szathmáry presented the Algren manuscript to the University of Iowa Libraries as the premier item in his superlative culinary manuscript collection. The University of Iowa Libraries and the University of Iowa Press are proud to inaugurate the Iowa Szathmáry Culinary Arts Series with *America Eats*, an account of midwestern foodways, customs, and lore.

ACKNOWLEDGMENTS

Chef Louis Szathmáry deserves credit for recognizing the importance of Nelson Algren's typescript of *America Eats* and making it available for study and eventual publication. At the State Historical Society of Iowa, Iowa City, Mary Bennett provided superb guidance to the photograph collections. Robert Tibbetts of the Ohio State University Libraries furnished helpful information from their Nelson Algren Collection.

Finally, I would like to express my appreciation to these colleagues at the University of Iowa Libraries for their encouragement and assistance with this project: Sheila Creth, Edward Shreeves, Robert Mc-Cown, Susan Hansen, Ann Ford, and Rijn Templeton.

The Buffalo Border

❦ ❦ ❦ ❦ ❦ ❦ ❦ ❦ ❦ ❦

THE FLOWERING SAVANNAS

If each of all of the races which have subsisted in the vast Middle West could contribute one dish to one great midwestern cauldron, it is certain that we'd have therein a most foreign and most gigantic stew: the grains that the French took over from the Indians and the breads that the English brought later, hotly spiced Italian dishes and subtly seasoned Spanish ones, the sweet Swedish soups and the sour Polish ones, and all the Old World arts brought to the preparing of American beefsteak and hot mince pie.

Such a cauldron would contain more than many foods; it would be, at once, a symbol of many lands and a melting pot for many peoples.

Many peoples, yet one people; many lands, one land.

In the old French time America's great inland plains were carpeted by a spiraling wild grass called bluestem. Among the bluestem grew the prairie wildflowers. In the fall the inland Indians set fire to the bluestem to provide pasturage for the buffalo in spring—the ranging shagskin herds that returned with each spring to the unstaked savannas. To the spiraling bluestem of the flowering savannas. By the time the French came such fires had stripped three-fourths of the plains of trees.

In October, by the rivers of the wilderness and among the rushes of the swamps, the French adventurers watched Illiniwek braves harvesting knotted stalks of wild oats. The Indians passed in canoes among the overhanging stalks to shake the wild grain down into the boats. The French saw that the Indians, as though taking on the autumn color of

1

Prairie scene. Courtesy of the Iowa Conservation Commission.

the bluestem country, wore blue-beaded moccasins and bright blue head-feathers and had the trick of turning autumn ears of yellow-brown corn into blue ears. With the wild oats they played no such tricks. They brought it back in the canoes, as brown as it grew, to their copper-brown women.

After cleaning the chaff, the women dried the oats on a wooden lattice by sustaining a fire beneath it for several days. They put the oats in skin bags, forced it into holes in the ground, treaded out the grain, winnowed it, reduced it to meal, boiled it in water, and seasoned it in bear grease. In the same fashion other Frenchmen watched the lean Menominees in the Wisconsin country harvest wild rice.

On the shores of Lake Superior Frenchmen found Chippewas living largely on fish, fresh in summer, dried or smoked in winter, and Chippewa squaws feeding their babies fish soup. Fish heads seasoned with maple sugar were a Chippewa delicacy. And beaver tails, because of their smooth fatness, were an especial treat.

The Chippewas boiled venison with wild rice or sliced it, roasted it, and pounded it out on a flat stone. Jerked and tenderized venison steaks they stored and packed in *makuks*, or birchbark boxes, the covers of which were sewn down with split spruce root. The fall-killed deer they dried in fire or wind, packed it in hide, and jerked the meat against the bitter lake winters.

Sometimes they cut venison into yet smaller slices, spread it out on birchbark, and stamped it into edibility. The braves were proud to do the stamping, for such work required strength and so was a brave's rightful task. Therefore the Chippewas called such meat, literally, foot-trodden meat.

The squaws performed other labors. When meat was needed for a trek, they lined a hole in the ground with hide, skin side out as with the wild oats, filled it with dried meat, and, with a stone for a pestle, pounded the meat until it was pulverized. When buffalo meat was used the result was called pemmican. Mixing the meat with fat or marrow and sometimes pounding cherries into it, they sealed it by pouring melted fat over the hide sacks. There it could keep for as long as three years. Such packs commonly weighed between one hundred and three hundred pounds.

The French *engagés* brought steel knives to the Chippewa nation to use instead of ribs or other bones of animals; clamshells were Chippewa spoons. Pointed sticks were employed to take meat out of a kettle when it was too hot to take with the fingers. Cups and all sorts of dishes were fashioned by this people from birchbark. In freshly cut birchbark vessels water could be heated before the bark was dry enough to catch fire.

The Chippewas customarily ate only once a day, usually about the middle of the morning. But if food was abundant they ate as frequently as their stomachs would permit. They might go in flush times to as many as seven feasts in a single day and at each be expected to eat all that was placed before them. When food was scarce, however, they, like other tribes, suffered severely, for they possessed no methods for storing food beyond the processing of pemmican.

Yet the explorer Coronado reported cultivated gardens and domesti-
cated turkeys among the Zunis. All the way east, across the sunburned
mesas, he found Indian gardens. He came up the borders of old Nebraska and on into dusty land and found the Kansas Indians in the
sandy Kansas bottoms gardening Indian corn. And growing a strange
dark gourd they called *askutasquash*, the same that the French named
pompon. The gourd that we today call simply squash.

And somewhere between Nebraska and Kansas, Coronado reported
tribes to be existing on "maize whereof they have great store, and also
small white peas and venison, which by all likelihood they feed upon
(though they may not) for we found many skins of deer, of hares, and
coneys. They eat the best cakes that I ever saw, and everybody generally
eats of them. They have the finest order and way to grind that we ever
saw in any place. And one Indian woman of the country will grind as
much as four women of Mexico."

It was from the Indian nations, of course, that the white men took
corn. They had expended hundreds of years in developing it out of a
seed-bearing grass. Eons before Columbus, the Indian was cultivating
this grass in both North and South America. Among some tribes, Coronado reported not only blue but red, yellow, black, and white ears colored for use in ceremonials. The secret of developing such colored ears
has to this date eluded the white man.

Coronado also found the Kansas Indians to possess a "most excellent
salt kernel." But of the Sioux it is said that as late as 1912 the older
members of the tribe had not, even by that late date, ever tasted salt.
Yet, though the Sioux used neither salt nor pepper, they seasoned meat
with wild ginger. And brewed a sweet wilderness tea from wintergreen
and raspberry leaves or little twigs of spruce. And in the long hot sum-
mers refreshed themselves with cold water into which a little maple
sugar had been dissolved.

Sioux living near the upper waters of the Minnesota River raised
small patches of corn and beans, but their principal vegetable was *tip-
sinna*, or Dakota turnip, eaten raw or roasted or boiled with buffalo
meat. Among the river rushes or in the shallow inland creeks, they too

Winnebago Indian woman in cornfield, Allamakee County, November 9, 1931.

harvested the wild rice. And, as with other Indian nations, roast dog was a delicacy reserved for feast days. They cooked it indifferently, without removing claws or hair.

"They feed themselves with such meats as the soil affords," an early journal reports, ". . . their meat is very well sodden and they make broth very sweet and savory. . . ."

Among this nation the French found beans, pumpkins, acorns, fresh and dried wild roots, bear fat, bulbs, and oil of the wild sunflower's seeds. Bread was baked by fire or sun and flattened on warm stones. In season, berries were plentiful; papayas and persimmons and, with the first frost, hickory nuts and walnuts. But mostly the Sioux lived by the fish of the streams, the wild geese and the wild pigeon, and all the game of the prairie groves.

Corn bread, still popular in both urban and rural sections of the Middle West, does not derive from either the journeycakes brought from England by the Puritans or from the richer breads of Virginia in the days of the Old Dominion. Midwestern corn bread is a direct descendant of the Indian ashcake, mixed from cornmeal and water, fashioned into thick cakes, and baked in the cinders and ashes of prairie camp fires.

In the years of the buckskin border this method of baking corn bread remained unmodified by the frontiersman. One legend has it that on an occasion when an unusually long train of Conestoga wagons was crossing the plains of Kansas, it was found necessary to separate into two trains. With but one frying pan and a single pot in the whole caravan, the division was accomplished by counting off those who preferred ashcake to boiled dumplings. Those who preferred ashcakes took the skillet; the ones who went for dumplings followed the pot.

Today corn bread and chicken with dumplings remain a favorite in Kansas. But an anonymous balladeer long ago warned all Nebraskans against the Kansas ashcake:

> Come, all young girls, pay attention to my noise.
> Don't fall in love with the Kansas boys.

For if you do your portion it will be
Ashcakes and antelope is all you'll see.

And further deprecated Kansas:

When they get hungry and go to make bread
They kindle a fire as high as your head,
Rake around the ashes and in they throw
The name they give it is "doughboy's dough."

When they go courting they take along a chair.
The first thing they say is, "Has your daddy killed a bear?"
The second thing they say when they sit down
Is, "Madam, your ashcake is baking brown."

In making bread, a thin sponge was made the night before, with yeast dissolved in lukewarm water, buckwheat flour, and enough additional water to make a thin paste. The batter bowl or crock was then covered with a lid and placed near the stove to rise overnight. If the night was quite cold, a piece of old blanket would be thrown over the crock just before going to bed to keep the heat in. In the morning the batter, all bubbly from fermentation, would be stirred thoroughly with more buckwheat flour and water and seasoned. Sometimes milk was used as part of the liquid.

Baked on a cast-iron griddle, the cakes were small and not over an eighth of an inch thick, brown on top, and crisp around the edges.

The residue of batter in the bowl was saved as a starter for the next morning's batch. After standing all day in the sun, it was again well fermented and ready to be mixed into another thin sponge.

"When I was single," a married minstrel mourned, "I eat biscuit an' pie. / Now I am married, / It's eat corn bread or die."

Such bread, like pemmican, would keep for a long time and was easily transported by men who lived on their feet.

Broiling was accomplished by putting meat on the end of a pointed stick and holding it over a fire. When the hunter cut a smooth stick and thrust it through the body of the bird or animal he had killed, he could rest the two ends of the stick on stones and roast the meat over the coals.

The Indian stick was replaced by a spit or iron rod to let the heat of the iron cook the inside of the roast. Finally, the cook learned to baste the meat with oil, water, or gravy collected in a dripping pan set under the spit.

The barbecue was adapted by the white buffalo hunters from the Indian method of barbecuing. Even pemmican was sometimes barbecued by adding to the jerked meat ground corn and bacon, cooking the mess together in steaming bear fat.

The modifications effected by the Indian and frontiersman upon each other's diet were reciprocal. The Indian taught the white man to exist in the wilderness, on the unstaked plains, and across the endless desert passes; in turn, the frontiersman instructed the Indian in the fastest known methods of getting blind drunk on barrel-whiskey.

For as little as one rabbit pelt a throw.

The frontiersman did, however, stabilize the Indian diet by improving on and inventing methods of storage. He built silos for the stored grain, established himself in one place whereat he could alternate crops against the hard midwestern winters. Though in all means of developing grain and providing against the future he was more thoughtful than the Indian, in the killing of wild game he was prodigal. Before the homesteaders had come, the great clouds of wild pigeons were gone, the buffalo were going, and the wilderness streams were fished dry. In killing he surpassed any Indian. For he took to it imaginatively, as he might go dancing, for the anticipated pleasure and the relating of it after the slaughter was done—till the plains were littered with buffalo carcasses, touched only by the fingers of the wind.

He desolated the Indian lands, then went on to destroy the food of his own sons, making square-dance songs all the while:

Oh, the hawk shot the buzzard and the buzzard shot the crow
And we'll rally 'round the canebrake to shoot the buffalo.

Woman feeding calf in front of small frame house.

It was not until the advent of the homesteaders, with all the caution that domestication brings, that some pause was put to the destruction. By that time the Indian was eating government rations from tins. And by the time of the War between the States, the white had modified the Indian's natural diet in more ways than one. In fact, he had just about put a stop to it altogether.

COONSKIN CARNIVAL

Before the land was laced by the railroads and the long fields bound by Sears Roebuck fencing, the prairies yielded abundant game. Deer and wild turkey wandered the land. Bee trees gave such tubs of honey that every prairie grove sheltered sugar camps. Corn was cultivated for use in johnnycake, corn mush, big hominy, ashcake, corn whiskey, corn pone, or the small loaves called corn dodgers.

A corn-dodger carnival in coonskin tatters came through the Cumberland into Illinois. Hungry movers from the settled seaboard, flintlock vagrants looking for a home. "I got a clock in my stomach, an' a watch in my head," one of them sang, "but I'm gettin' superstitious 'bout my hog an' bread."

To many, the Illinois country looked like home. They built log cabins and exchanged their coonskins for wide farmers' straws and overalls. The flintlocks hung rusting on the cabin walls. The land was cleared and fields were sewn. Rain came, sun came, the land was bounded.

Beside each cabin, in the squaw winters, they dug a pit eight or ten feet long and about six feet deep in which to store vegetables against the snow. Potatoes, cabbage, and turnips were covered with straw and the entire pit covered with about three feet of earth, leaving a small opening near the center for the heat of the vegetables to escape. Sometimes during extreme cold one would have to start a fire to thaw out the frost so as to get at the food; this very seldom occurred as the heat of the vegetables kept the earth from freezing.

Cabin chairs were three- or four-legged stools, tables had four legs but were made from puncheon, and the silverware consisted of jackknives or a butcher knife. Boardinghouse guests were frequently requested to bring their own cutlery. Plates and dishes were of tin or pewter, and often wooden bowls, known as noggins, served when metal containers were not available. Or sometimes even thin wooden shingles served for plates. Drinking cups made from gourds were common.

Corn-dodger days are occasionally recalled in Illinois by corn-dodger dinners, but in the early pioneer times they were the mainstay of the average man's diet. Six days a week the coonskin folk ate them. Corn dodgers were baked in a skillet to such a consistency that a wit of the era once observed that "you could knock down a Texas steer with a chunk of the stuff or split an end-board at forty yards off-hand." One tune complained:

My clothes is all ragged, as my language is rough,
My bread is corn dodgers both solid and tough,
But yet I am happy, and live at my ease
On sorghum molasses, bacon, and cheese.

Only on Sunday, if all the children had been good, was there any variation in this corn-dodger diet. The Lord's Day brought biscuits and preserves to the righteous. And a casual visit by a circuit-riding preacher always called for the best a homesteader could lay on the table. Perhaps it was some such visit that inspired an anonymous hired man, when requested to say grace, to ad-lib his own lines—with one eye on the table:

Oh Lord of Love who art above
Thy blessings have descended:
Biscuits and tea for supper I see
When mush and milk was intended.

For mush and milk, like corn and salt pork, were Illinois staples year-round.

In winter, selected kernels of corn were treated with lye, which removed the hull, after which the grains were boiled or fried. This was big hominy and was a wholesome, satisfying article of diet. Farmers would save all their wood ashes until they had a sufficient quantity, then would cover these with water till the combination formed the lye. The lye water would then be filled with shelled white corn and left till the grains swelled and popped open. The corn kernels were then scrubbed over a washboard with the bare hands to remove the hulls. Sometimes a preliminary cooking was necessary to finish the removal of the hulls. Then several more tubs of water were used to wash the corn to get the heavy lye out. Much trouble was endured by the housewife to get this job finished. Nowadays canned lye is used, but old-timers say the hominy is not as good.

Hoe-cakes, originated by Virginians, were made by spreading a thin

Corn shocks in field, ca. 1904. W. A. Warren Collection.

mixture of cornmeal over a hot iron plate or on a board placed in front of the fire.

> Wake up, Jacob, day's a-breakin',
> Fryin' pan's on an' hoe-cake bakin',
> Bacon in the pan, coffee in the pot,
> Git up now an' git it while it's hot.

The first inquiry a landlord of those years made of a guest at meal-time was simply, "Well, stranger, what'll ye take, wheat bread 'n chicken-fixins or common-doin's?" Common-doin's was corn bread, just as corn pone was commonly knick-knacks. Of which it is told that a settler, falling ill, called his best friend to his bedside and asked, "I want you to do one thing for me—take some corn to mill and get it ground, and make me some knick-knacks or I'll surely die."

A beverage popular with early Illinois settlers was a drink known as stew, consisting of a mixture of water, sugar, whiskey, allspice, and butter, served steaming hot. When pioneer schoolmasters followed the custom of celebrating the final day of the school term with parents and pupils, the oldest girl of the class was given the task of preparing the stew. Occasionally instructors partook too freely and became "stewed"—a phrase handed down to the present day.

Genuine tea was both difficult to obtain and very expensive; many substitute brews were used by the pioneers. Among the more popular substitutes were those made from sycamore chips and red-root leaves. In Mercer County the red-root leaves were first dried in a dutch oven and then pulverized by rolling between the hands. When brewed and sweetened with honey, this drink was called grub hyson. Wheat parched and ground served for coffee. And early settlers agreed that the "hardest difficulty of all" was to teach Yankees to drink sour milk and to use honey for butter.

The homely wisdom of Illinois pioneers prescribed that children be passed through a hole in the trunk of a hollow tree to cure "short growth"; hogs must be slaughtered at certain times of the moon or the bacon would shrink; babies must be weaned at certain times of the zodiac; the madstone, a small bone from the heart of a deer, was a valued antidote for hydrophobia or snakebite; certain persons "blew the fire out of a burn," arrested hemorrhage, or cured erysipelas by uttering mysterious charms; a pan of water under the bed was used to check night sweats; bleeding was the sovereign remedy for fits, loss of consciousness, fever, and many other ills; and in eruptive fevers, especially measles, where the eruption was delayed, a tea made of sheep's dung, popularly known as nany tea, was a household remedy.

Illinoisans got their drinking water from springs. Those who came later dug wells, some of which failed to afford the needed supply of water for drinking, cooking, and other purposes. After one or two such disappointments, the property owner would sometimes call in the local waterwitch. The waterwitch held a divining rod in his hands, which would be drawn down by some mysterious force when held over a vein of water. For this purpose a forked piece of witch hazel was usually selected. With a prong of this tightly grasped in each hand, his arms extended at full length, the point of the fork pointing upward, the waterwitch would slowly and gravely walk over a spot where it was desired to sink a well. In the event water was found where the water-witch directed, the discovery was heralded as proof of his powers.

Very few of the early settlers had cisterns, and rainwater was obtained by catching it in a barrel into which the water from the eaves of the house was conveyed by a long, slanting board. In warm weather, if this rainwater was not used soon it would come to be filled with "wiggle-tails."

Following winter diet came spring sickness. Nearly everybody used to be sick because of the lack of green stuff to eat. In the spring the papers carried daily advertisements for sarsaparilla "to cure boils, sluggishness, thick blood, and other ailments resulting from heavy winter food."

"The matter in the blood is thoroughly vitiated," one journal advised its readers, "and improving it must be a matter of time. Spring diet should do the work of medicine, largely. First in importance are salads of all sorts."

Hanging from the cabin rafters would be festoons of dried apples, dried pumpkins, dried peaches, peppers, bunches of sage for seasoning sausage, bunches of pennyroyal to "sweat" the sick, and bunches of boneset to "break the ager."

> There's bread and cheese upon the shelf.
> If you want any, just help yourself.

A product strictly of the central prairies relished by Cavalier and Yankee alike was the vinegar pie. Early Illinoisans felt keenly the absence of native fruit. Along toward spring their systems developed a craving for something tart. To satisfy the craving, ingenious housewives invented the vinegar pie—vinegar, molasses, water, a little nutmeg, and flour enough to bring the mixture to the consistency of a custard.

Covered wagon pulled by single ox, Mitchell's store, Maquoketa.
Paul Juhl Collection.

When baked in a pie tin, the resulting product was much relished and remained a favorite springtime dessert until young orchards coming into bearing provided real fruit pies to take its place.

Going to mill was nearly always done on horseback. A sack of wheat or shelled corn would be put on a horse with the grain divided so there would be an equal amount in each end, and on this a boy would be mounted and started for the water mill, which was never more than four or five miles away. When he arrived there, the miller would take the sack into the mill and pour its contents into the hopper, from which it ran in between the two millstones, one of which, connected with a waterwheel in the stream beneath, revolved while the other was stationary. Both were sharply grooved properly to crush and grind the grain that passed between them. For this purpose the miller took a toll, that is, a certain percentage of the grain or, as is usually said in this sense, the grist.

LAND OF MIGHTY BREAKFASTS

Following the Civil War, a considerable migration into the lumber country of Michigan occurred. Houses were rudely built in these areas, and settlement was transitory. Hundreds of small communities would spring up, only to disappear when the land was cut over and the sawmills removed to new timberland. Such conditions did not encourage variation in diet; food monotony reached a new high in lumber-operating sections of the state during the last three decades of the nineteenth century.

Paul Bunyan felt there were two kinds of Michigan lumber-camp cooks, the Baking Powder Buns and the Sourdough Stiffs. One Sourdough Sam belonged to the latter school. He made everything but coffee out of sourdough. He had only one arm and one leg, the other members having been lost when his sourdough barrel blew up.

The hyperbole serves to emphasize a truth. The sourdough pancake has always been a favorite among lumberjacks everywhere. To the camp cook a continuous supply of sourdough is an indispensable part of camp equipment, and he is never without his batch of starter. The starter is a portion of dough reserved from previous mixtures and stored in the kind of barrel that proved disastrous to Sourdough Sam. Zealously guarded, the starter can be kept for weeks in ordinary temperatures.

The night before the pancakes are to be fried, the cook assembles his batter, using the starter as a leavening agent. Flour and water are added to the starter, and the mixture is left near the stove to rise. By morning it is a light and frothy mass, smelling pungently of fermentation. After

Cook wagon at campsite, South Dakota, ca. 1900. Brinton Collection.

reserving from the batch a starter for the next morning's pancakes, the cook adds salt, sugar, eggs, a little fat, and a pinch of soda. He pours large spoonfuls of the batter on a huge, fire-blackened griddle, abundantly greased with smoking pork rind and very hot. Then, after the griddle cake has fried a few moments, he flips it expertly and it's as good as done.

In the old camps it was customary for the cook to install near the door of the shanty a crock containing sourdough batter in various stages of fermentation. Into the crock went all leftover batter and scraps of bread, doughnuts, cake, or pancakes, which quickly attained the semiliquid consistency of the batter.

Standing in a box sled among steaming kettles of beans, beef stew, and tea, the bull cook drove over a road to a central point in the woods to blow his dinner horn. The call carried five miles through the snowy forest. Then he howled like an Irish wolf: "Ye-ow! 's goin' to waste." The men swarmed toward the box sled from every direction. Though they ate around a big fire of slash, the beans froze on their plates and the tea froze in their whiskers.

At night they came into camp stamping with cold and grim with hunger. In the cookhouse the long tables were loaded with food— smoking platters of fresh mush, bowls of mashed potatoes, piles of pancakes and pitchers of corn syrup, kettles of rich brown beans, pans of prunes, dried peaches, rice pudding, rows of apple pies. The big camps fed the men bountifully and well.

> Run here, men, it's bilin' hot,
> Sam 'n Dave's both eatin' out the pot.
> Old Uncle Jake says, "I'll be damn,
> If I can't get a foreleg I'll take a ham."

The jacks ate silently, with great speed. If a greenhorn was tempted to make conversation, he was reminded by a placard on the wall: "No talking at the table."

The cook was the king bee of the camp. He was well paid and well worth his pay, handling prodigious quantities of food, baking, roasting, frying, stewing for a hundred men who ate like horses, feeding them lavishly on an allowance of thirty cents a day per man.

The preparation of beans verged on ritual. A deep hole was dug on one side of the fire and filled with glowing embers. When the beans had been soaked for twenty-four hours, they were taken out and scalded. With deliberation the cook now chose the right kind of onion and placed it on the bottom of the pot. Then the beans were poured in until the pot was filled within six inches of the top. Slices of fat pork were laid across this, a sufficiency of molasses was poured upon the whole, and the pot sealed. The embers were now taken from the hole in the floor and the pot inserted. All space around the sides was filled and packed with hot coals and the bean hole covered up. The fire was made over it and kept burning twenty-four hours, when the cooking was complete. This made a rich and golden breakfast dish.

Beans and salt pork—generally sowbelly—were the substantialities of the menu, and fried cakes made the dessert. Upon this unadorned diet the men thrived, for there was little sickness among them.

Taken at random from a long list of meals served at small Michigan boardinghouses, hotels, and even private homes, one meal that appears quite typical consisted of bread, fried salt pork, onions, homegrown lettuce, and tea. This was for supper, but breakfast was much the same, with the possible exception of onions. Those who carried a lunch to work took bread, pork, onions, and lettuce and cooked dried beans in a tin pail. Such pails were more often than not of a five-quart capacity and were filled to the brim.

The tin dinner pail was the pivot point around which the day revolved—that and the water pail. The latter reposed on a bench near the schoolhouse door with a tin dipper either in it or hanging from a nearby nail. Just above was a shelf for the dinner pails. The opening of the dinner pails in the country school upon the very instant of dismissal was a time for conjecture and speculation. Barter and trade ran high at the dinner hour, and those children whose mothers held the highest reputation in the culinary arts were likely to go home at night in a state of hungry bitterness.

As the tin tops were pried off of the pails, released odors often gave out advance information regarding contents. That of sour pickles predominated, injudiciously mixed with the aroma of chocolate cake or fried cakes. Fresh bread and red-brown spice cake richly embedded with raisins were fair plunder for the cunning speculator. Often there would be an addition to the well-packed pail—perhaps a small glass of jelly with one of Grandmother's old silver spoons to eat it with. Or a little jar of baked beans with another of piccalilli or chili sauce. The bread was of more than generous thickness, maybe a hunk of some kind of cold meat, a hard-boiled egg, a piece of pie, a doughnut, and— for most—the inevitable pickle. If there was room for an apple it went in, otherwise it went into a coat pocket.

Michigan house-raisings were conducted to the accompaniment of a great deal of liquor, and in some quarters it was not considered proper

Schoolchildren with lunch pails, Palo Alto County, April 15, 1909.
E. M. Clark Collection.

to have a raising without it. When Indians were among those invited, special care had to be exercised in permitting them access to the barrel, as they had a tendency to drink almost as heavily as the whites.

> Whiskey by the barrel,
> Sugar by the pound,
> A great big bowl to put it in
> And a spoon to stir it around.

It was a day of mighty breakfasts, and Michigan was the state for it.

> Come an' see what yo' got
> On yo' breakfast table:
> Ram, ham, chick'n 'n mutton,

Ef yo' don't come now
You won't get nuttin'.

When the lumber boom died, Michigan lumberjacks packed up their axes and families and joined the great westward migrations of the sixties and seventies. "Remember beans before you start," they were warned, "Likewise dried beef and ham. / Beware of venison, damn the stuff, / It's oftener a ram."

Kitchens were accordingly huge in proportion to the ones which city-bred generations know. Much of rural family life was conducted in the kitchens. Breakfast was generally served about six o'clock in the morning, and the meal was barely over before the women plunged into the business of preparing dinner. Dinners, too, were lusty affairs: from the cellar would come squash, rutabagas, cabbage, and some canned fruit and pickles. There was fresh cornmeal so recent from the mill that it had not yet become infested with weevils. A roaring wood fire in a stove that stood high on four legs and that had an apron on the front as a resting place for an iron spider was the axis around which revolved the kitchen program.

Donation parties were interesting events in the lives of Michigan people who lived at widely separated distances from each other. Everybody brought something. Competition ran in a manner much the same as at a county fair, because all articles were open and labeled with the name of the donor. It was about the only time each person had the opportunity to estimate the contents of the other fellow's cellar and smokehouse. Great hams, huge slabs of bacon, sowbellies, and sausages of various kinds were strewn here and there on a long table.

Potatoes in huge sacks, apples in rough board barrels, dry beans by the peck, and other items from the cellar under the house or from the root cellar—cabbage, turnips, parsnips, and squash. The women came in for their share of attention by presenting handiwork. Jellies and jams, apple butter, pickles, and large jars of canned fruits were exhibited before critical neighbors, who knew from experience just how a pickle

Woman coming out of fruit cellar. Henrietta Harris Collection.

should be placed in a jar to avoid display of a white spot and who knew how to select a cucumber in order to bring out its best qualities. Such neighbors also knew how to counteract the ultimate appearance of wrinkles that enlarge the warts on a pickle or the magnifying effect of glass on the fuzz of pickled peaches.

The men took this occasion to show off the results of their husbandry. Well-selected potatoes—not a little one in an entire sack—carefully graded apples, corn, both dry for stock feed or ground into meal, the biggest squashes they grew the summer before, and a variety of other commodities that would excite the envy of a modern storekeeper were all there on exhibition for the edification of their neighbors.

This spirit of friendly rivalry was not only an outlet for these people but, incidentally, provided the minister with what it takes.

Michigan farmers years ago used to meet for a turkey shoot held by a farmer who had a yard full of turkeys to sell and devised this method of disposing of them. A pit was dug from which to fire, and a turkey was placed in a box with only the head sticking out. The object was to shoot the head off at a range of eighty rods, with a price of twenty-five cents for ten shots, on the average. Expert hunters who had proved their marksmanship on previous shoots were restricted to five shots for the same price, but even then they were often good enough with the use of their guns to bag half a wagon load of birds.

At these meets, when it became too dark for further shooting, cold roast turkey, pumpkin pie, and cider made a grand supper for farmers and their friends who went in for dancing to the tune of hornpipes and fiddle.

Festivals in the Fields

❦ ❦ ❦ ❦ ❦ ❦ ❦ ❦ ❦ ❦ ❦ ❦

"We shuk an' bresh'd the dry corn silks offen our cloes an' went inter the house. . . . In the middel o' the long tabel thet tuk up the senter o' the room stud a roasted shote thet look'd mos'es nateral es life, wi' a yer o' corn in its mouth an' a ring o' tumblers full o' biled custard wi' littel dabs o' red jell on top a surlin' roun' it. An' piled on over' whars' on the outside o' this 'ere wus ven'zon an' wile turkey an' jole an' cabbage an' pumpkin butter an' cowcumber pickles an' biskits an' smokin' hot corn aigy bred an' stacks o' all kins' o' pies an' cakes know'd ter pi'neers an' a small o' fride ham an' coffee a purvadin' thet putt on the cap sheef an' made us ten times hongrier'n ever."

The French were the first, and the quickest, to learn the wilderness ways from the Indian hunters who fished the secret rivers of that lost and secret wilderness: the Huron and Illiniwek, the Pottawattomi and Fox. Their arrows in the aspen leaves first taught the French, then all the races that followed. Till the teaching was no longer by arrow but by the peacepipe and the banquet board. By the ripening maize and the harvest festival.

To the Indian, the ripening of the corn marked the beginning of the new year and the end of the old. Among many tribes, at this time of year no tribe member would eat of or even handle any part of the harvest until the Festival of First Fruits had been conducted. This was a forerunner of the white man's husking bees and harvest homes.

Other tribes, before going on the warpath, avoided all meat. But the Kansas Indians in preparing for war conducted a feast in the chief's hut, of which the principal dish was roast dog. This was a custom in the tradition of homeopathic magic common to all peoples of the globe in all stages of civilization, the theory being that an animal capable, as the dog was supposed to be, of letting himself be destroyed in defense of his master must necessarily inspire an equal courage in the eater. Upon a similar assumption, the Sioux reduced to powder the hearts of valiant enemies, hoping thus to appropriate the dead man's gallantry. Or, when through eating, wiped his hands on his feet to lend them speed.

In the old French time the voyageurs sat at roast-dog feasts, clothed as colorfully as the blue-feathered braves themselves. They wore shirts and waistcoats of cotton, blue cloth or deer-skin trousers, and blue-beaded moccasins of bright Indian weave. In winter they wore long woolen coats with blue hoods attached which in wet weather or cold were drawn up over the head. And the head was commonly covered with a blue cotton handkerchief folded as a turban.

They learned not only to hunt and dress like the Indian but to eat like him. Marquette pronounced the wild oats or the *folles avoines* of as delicate a flavor as French-cooked rice. The precooked fish and buffalo meat served him by the Peoria Indians on the banks of the Mississippi he found both strengthening and palatable, and sagamité, mortar-pounded cornmeal flavored with berries and fried in bear grease, he pronounced delicious.

LaSalle's men ate heartily of a bear-meat feast tendered them by the Peorias. The Illiniwek fed Henri de Tonti of the best they had, though there came a time when he was reduced to digging with his one good hand the wild onions on the banks of the Chicago River.

A food custom peculiar to the Sioux was that of the Virgin Feast, a banquet conducted to resolve the truth or falsity of tribal scandal. When such scandal, concerning a young woman of the tribe, reached the ears of the girl's mother, the mother commanded the daughter to cook rice and to invite the other maidens of the tribe to partake of it. These young women would appear with the crimson circle of virginity painted on each cheek, seat themselves in a semicircle, and each be served a bowl of rice. Then a circular boulder painted red was placed

Prairie chickens with hay.

about ten feet distant and a knife plunged into the ground before it. The young men of the band then stood about with deadpan expressions, watching the maidens eat. If none of the youths spoke and the meal was finished without interruption, the maiden was vindicated and the gossip halted. But if one of the bucks had his doubts, he stepped forward, seized the girl by the hand, pulled her out of the ring, and made his charges point-blank. She had the right of swearing, by the circular stone and the plunged blade, to her innocence: this went a considerable distance toward vindication but was not considered conclusive. If her accuser persisted, an altercation ensued, upon which final tribal sentiment was formed.

The Sioux around St. Paul adapted the French custom of making calls on New Year's Day and receiving cakes, wines, and kisses. The Indians called it the kissing day and were inclined to make their calls very early in the morning, braves and squaws presenting themselves together, receiving equal gifts and equal kisses from the St. Paul householders.

On New Year's Eve it was the custom of the young men of the French colony around Cahokia, Illinois, to assemble dressed in masquerade costumes and each provided with a bucket, sack, basket, or other article for the carrying of solid or liquid provisions. About nine o'clock in the evening they started on the rounds of the homes, singing "La Guignolée" and receiving sugar, coffee, lard, candles, flour, maple syrup, ratafia, eggs, meat, and poultry. If a householder who was able to give refused, he commonly had his chicken house stripped clean.

And six days later, on the evening of the feast of Epiphany, the maidens of the town were invited by the youths to bake pancakes. The supplies gathered on New Year's Eve were then brought out to provide the feast.

On such holidays the French, both of Minnesota and of Illinois, fed the local Indians on anything and everything they had handy. But especially in southern Illinois on *galettes sauvages* or *croquecignolles*. These were two varieties of doughnuts, both made of the same ingredients but the latter being large, oblong in shape, and slit several times all the way through beginning about an inch from each end, with alternate sections raised. They were familiarly called tangled breeches. The *galettes sauvages* were about half the size of the *croquecignolles* and slit through three times. Sections were not raised, the slits taking the place of the hole in the common present-day doughnut.

The French also fashioned a tart called *pâté marraine* or Godmother's tart. For this, dough was rolled as in preparing pie crust and cut out in the form and size of a big plate. One kind of fruit was placed on half of the shaped dough, and the other side of the dough was punctured, as in ordinary fruit pies. This side was then folded over the fruit and the

Grain stacks on the Henry F. Came farm, Prairieburg. Kintzle Collection.

edges crimped to keep juice from escaping. Such tarts were given the godchildren upon visits to the godparents' home as something especially for godchildren.

Among other dishes which the Indian learned to eat from the hospitable French were crepes, or pancakes, and brioche, a coffee cake. For this, an exceptionally rich dough was used, but only moderately sweet. It was usually shaped in rings, snails, or braids and covered with nuts or fruits. It was made up with butter instead of with the usual vegetable shortening. This was a breakfast bread served with strong black coffee. (For original and tested recipes, see the last two chapters.)

The French in all parts of the Middle West have had a penchant for bouillon parties, from the first settlements down to the present. At such occasions as card parties, eaten with crackers or bread, bouillon still replaces coffee in southern Illinois among the French.

Another old French custom of the same area still lends an added zest to holiday suppers by using in the bouillon chickens stolen by one member of the community from another. To invite a neighbor to dine on his own fowl is considered a social grace, to be caught prowling in the henhouse is something else.

The French still make a stew in southern Illinois, cooked all day over a slow fire, called potpourri and reported to be more savory than American stew, its essence being its treatment by such spices as thyme and bay leaf.

It was a Frenchman, too, who was instrumental in originating burgoo, a stew still popular in the Lincoln country and western Kentucky. His name was Gus Jaubert, and he was associated with the Confederate raider John Hunt Morgan. On an occasion when Morgan had conducted a successful supply raid, Jaubert was commissioned to cook the spoils. Into a five hundred–gallon kettle used for making gunpowder he threw beans, chickens, potatoes, corn, cabbage, tomatoes, and everything else he could find. The result was neither a soup nor a stew but possessed the best qualities of both. And has since been a favorite in the Kentucky country on occasions when a large crowd of people is to be fed. But Morgan County in Illinois is today, appropriately enough, the country's biggest burgoo county. It is also common enough in Jersey, Greene, and Macoupin counties.

In these counties, a harvest-home festival today requires that all foods served be raised within county bounds. After the supper, the dancing begins—square dancing to the mountain tunes that came to the Illinois country long ago:

> Oh I want none of your weevily wheat,
> I want none of your barley,
> I'll take some flour and a half an hour
> And bake a cake for Charley.

After the dancing and eating are done, the leftover food is packed in bushel baskets for distribution among the poor. There have been harvest-home suppers downstate when enough was left over to fill sixty-five such baskets.

The country around East St. Louis, although traditionally French, is now largely dominated by Americans of German extraction. Their influence can be seen in *Wurst Markt* dinners: literally, sausage market. Such a dinner consists of homemade pork sausage, mashed potatoes, all kinds of vegetables, and bread and fruit pies.

The homesteaders lived lives of isolation, but once or twice a year a box social was held at the local schoolhouse. Each young woman brought a box of food. These were auctioned, the buyer sharing the food and becoming the partner for the evening of the young lady whose box he bought, sharing the same schoolroom desk and seat. The owners of the boxes were supposed to be secret. Somehow, though, it nearly always leaked out, and that of the most popular belle often fetched a substantial price. The food usually was crisp fried chicken, several pieces of pie, some slices of cake and not infrequently included some homemade candy and a few bought red apples. But the food wasn't the thing. It was the social get-together that made the box social important.

In neighborhoods where social contact is still difficult, the box social is awaited from year to year. Various superstitions have grown out of these occasions: "fancy box, homely girl" or "too much time spent on the outside, not enough on the inside."

Cakewalks, while not strictly eating occasions, are a related activity. Here, numbers are marked off on a circle on a floor and competitors pay for the privilege of walking around the circle to music. When the music stops the number on a cake is revealed, and the person standing on the corresponding number on the floor captures the cake.

Sauerkraut Day is the largest single-day celebration in Illinois. The town of Forreston, for example, has entertained no less than 20,000 visitors at one time, with fourteen barrels of kraut, a ton of wienies, 30,000 buns, and gallons of coffee.

In central Illinois as in other sections of the country, the immigration of foreigners has exerted a strong influence on what the people eat. Sauerkraut and sauerbraten are today common American foods. In communities with a predominant Scandinavian population, fish pud-

Putting up Amana sauerkraut, Homestead, 1920s.

dings and *bakkels* have gained some popularity. The Italians have given us ravioli and gnocchi, the Hungarians goulash and *galuska*, and the Greeks a variety of tasty combination dishes. Every midwestern city of any size has its restaurant where chop suey is served by Chinese, and in communities where there are large numbers of Russians and Armenians, we find adherents who speak very highly of the borsch and *bitochky smetance* of the former and the kebab of the latter.

Along the Wabash, after Yankee and Cavalier had pressed the French adventurers west, Hoosier homesteaders began developing festal customs after the manner of all rural folk who remain in one country for more than one generation.

An apple peelin', for example, was as good an excuse as any for a party.

Upon arrival, each peeler was given a crock of apples and a paring knife. A ten- to twenty-gallon stone jar was placed in the center of a group of five to eight persons. Here the apples which were peeled, cored, and quartered were deposited.

As each peeler finished his batch, the crock was removed and he was handed another full one. All participated in this except the passers, who were usually the host and hostess. The peeling usually ended about 9:30 in the evening, and by this time jars and buckets stood brimming with apples. Each unmarried man kept strict tab on the number of crocks of apples he had peeled, because the winner could kiss any girl he chose. Which invariably brought forth much giggling and good-humored teasing.

Immediately upon finishing the peelin', the men went into the parlor, moved the furniture into the sitting room, took up the homemade rag rug, sprinkled generous quantities of cornmeal and salt over the wide boards of the floor, grouped chairs in one corner for the fiddle, French harp, and "gittar" players, calling out: "Partners to your places, hook up your back bend and tighten your braces."

The day after the peelin', two or three neighborwomen would come over to cook the apple butter. This was done in the backyard in a big copper kettle sitting on four stones over a log fire and stirred with ladles eighteen feet long.

After cooking the butter all day, as a final touch the exact amount of clove oil was dropped into it, and this gave it an indefinable flavor not to be duplicated by factory butter. Then it was sealed in hot, sterile glass jars, cooled, and finally stored in the underground fruit cellar.

Related to the peelin's were stirrings. The hostess of the stirring prepared great kettles of cider which were kept boiling hot. Guests prepared apples which were put in the boiling cider and stirred until apple butter was achieved.

Pumpkin butter was made by boiling the pumpkin in a big kettle, then squeezing the juice out in a press and straining and boiling it down. Perhaps it would be thickened some with apples. They spread it on a piece of bread and thought it was the only butter in the world.

Grease from bears, deer, and coons was often rendered into candles,

Hog butchering, ca. 1913.

but when short of candles there was often nothing better than some grease in a dish with a rag set up in the middle. Coon grease was thought especially good for boots.

Following apple picking, bean threshing (with flails), corn husking, Indian summer, and the fall plowing came butchering time. The rites and ceremonies of hog killing naturally occurred after snappy weather had set in so that the pork could be kept fresh longer, which gave to the heating of huge cauldrons of water a certain element of coziness as well as the eternal thrill of fire building. Then there was the sharpening of the knives and the setting up of heavy planks on wooden horses, upon which the scalded hog was laid for the divestment of his hairy covering.

Housework was hustled out of the way and indoor preparations made beforehand as far as possible, for the housewife's share in the activities was but secondary to the outside drama. Bread, pies, and doughnuts were made and pans of beans baked so the stove would be left free

Monroe Adams family and friends at reunion, 1904. W. A. Warren Collection.

for the chief performance. Once the kill was over, fuel was added to the fire, knives were tested along leathern thumbs, and tubs and pans made ready to receive the entrails.

The huge quivering mass was then carried into the kitchen and placed on a table. Over this the housewife bent, to "strip the innards" or "riddle the guts." The fat from these was "tried out" in one kettle and rendered in another.

The advent of spareribs was one of the anticipated seasonal events, like dandelion greens in spring and sweet corn in summer. They came with the first severe freeze of early winter, when butchering time brought a welcome change to the meat diet, as did a mess of greens after a winter of potatoes and cabbage, and bespoke not only a delectable treat in themselves but a round of family dinners and neighborly exchange. For the farmers of a community usually made of butchering a succession of events in order to help each other with the work and to keep the feast of fresh meat going as long as possible.

The family reunion is another old Indiana custom, dating from the calico and blue jeans era. On a Sunday in July or August, fifteen or twenty will be scheduled in the public parks and churchyards of every county seat in the state.

This show really belongs to the mothers, who do most of the work, from organizing to cooking to riding herd on the children. Their part begins early in the morning—or perhaps even the day before—for it is almost universal for each family to bring along the food it will consume and a little extra besides.

If the reunion is being held in a public park, chances are that somebody has brought along a baseball and bat. The men and older boys troop off to the diamond (or cow pasture) and start a vigorous but necessarily brief game of baseball, during which the elders prove to themselves that they're just as spry as ever and the youngsters play all the key positions. The real veterans find or improvise a horseshoe court and pitch horseshoes.

While the ball game is still in full swing and the horseshoe pitchers are still trying for ringers, a little group of men may drift off to a convenient spot behind a building or in a clump of trees. There they stand solemnly and talk in low tones while Uncle John or Cousin Ned opens a bottle of whiskey. In times past it would have been pure Jasper County corn distilled in Uncle John's back lot, but today the art of moonshining is almost gone from the Hoosier hills. There's a drink around and pipes are lighted. But the drinking is quiet and usually slight, for the family reunion is dominated too thoroughly by the older women. For the most part, the presence of the bottle remains a closely guarded secret, betrayed only by Grandpa's insistence on telling the same story three times.

The younger children, in the meantime, are standing shyly at a re-

Men enjoying refreshments, Iowa City, ca. 1915. Courtesy of Henry Louis.

spectful distance from the main table, eyeing the food with wistful glances and trying to remember which of their fellows are the first cousins from Elwood.

When the baseball game has died away and the whiskey has been downed, dinner is ready and the entire clan assembles. The meat platters are first to move—chicken rolled in flour and fried in shallow fat to a rich, crisp brown, baked ham, beef roasted thoroughly to a heavy, tender darkness, gravied meat loaf kept hot for serving on a big camp-range. Chicken is the favorite with ham, beef, and meat loaf following in that order, but most plates receive at least two different kinds of meat.

The vegetables which follow include potatoes—creamed, scalloped, mashed, and chopped into salad—baked beans, green beans, lima beans, scalloped corn, sliced tomatoes, and fresh or pickled beets. Flanking them are deviled eggs, coleslaw, cottage cheese, and an end-

less variety of homemade pickles, sauces, relishes, jellies, jams, preserves, butters, and savories. Served at the same time is coffee, no matter how hot the day, poured in an endless stream from the spouts of
great coffeepots wielded by tireless women.

When a slacking off in the first rush of eating is indicated by the
gradual resumption of conversation, the servers start a second general
attack, urging everyone to have another helping of everything. Then,
when only the most hardy are still chewing away on chicken legs or
wishbones, the cakes are cut—angel food, devil's food, banana, marble,
sponge, coconut, orange, burnt sugar, and lazy daisy. These are followed by pumpkin, cherry, apple, mince, peach, blackberry, and custard pies.

Isolated communities in remote sections of southern Indiana still
maintain the pioneer custom of celebrating Independence Day by a
public meeting and barbecue. Bear meat and venison, the customary
main course, are today supplanted by barbecued beef and mutton. And
whereas the pioneers roasted the whole carcass on a spit, today it is
roasted in sections. A baseball game and fireworks usually follow.

Other Indiana communities still observe the pioneer custom of holding a pitch-in dinner on the occasion of a funeral. While the burial service is taking place, neighborwomen clear the house of all indication of
sickness and death and have a meal prepared for the mourners upon
their return. Every effort is made on such an occasion to avoid reminis-
cence of the deceased.

In southern Indiana as well as in southern Illinois, chicken is still
referred to as the gospel bird. This is a hangover from days when
circuit-riding preachers came visiting. It was customary to serve the
gospel man a chicken, hence the name.

Once in a while a sale lends spice to the Indiana farm life. The sale
may be the result of a man's "gettin' in debt," but usually it occurs when
someone is moving away or a family is broken up by death.

The sale is advertised a week or two beforehand by posters, and the
people will come to it from a distance of eight or ten miles. Sometimes
there are more than five hundred men at a single sale. It's an all-day

Funeral near Meroa, Mitchell County. Courtesy of Mary Noble.

affair, and at noon the folks who are selling out furnish everyone with a free lunch of bologna, crackers, coffee, and cheese.

The women at lunchtime set out food for the spectators and buyers in a barnyard buffet on plank tables where everyone reaches for free food. Years ago this free food was almost a necessity, since the farmers came for miles in a wagon or other open conveyance and since most of the sales were held in the late fall or early spring when the weather was severe.

Closely connected to the field festivals are those occasions which serve in rural areas to recall the pioneer past.

In Nebraska, for example, an Old Settlers' Picnic offers old-timers a chance to reminisce, as it offers the younger folks an opportunity to play games and to go courting.

Such picnics are held under great shade trees in the park at the edge of town. Long wooden tables are spread with white cloths and the food placed on them, and each person helps himself. Foods are prepared

Picnic near Waterloo; J. P. King, photographer. Paul Juhl Collection.

several days in advance except for the hot dishes. A large brick fireplace and oven combined supplies piping hot baked potatoes, sizzling sausages, hamburgers, and grilled steaks. The children are allowed one side of the fireplace to roast wieners and marshmallows. Potato salads are always in evidence, especially a Bulgarian recipe of potatoes, hard-boiled eggs, lettuce, and tomatoes, the whole well seasoned with garlic and garnished with thin slices of red and green peppers. Heaping bowls of ripe sliced tomatoes are placed every few inches across the table; other bowls are laden with fresh sliced cucumbers. Sweet pickles, dill pickles, bread and butter pickles, pickled peaches, pears, and crab apples by the gallon wait in crocks. Then there are coleslaws, mixed-vegetable salads, fruit salads, and gaily colored pickled eggs. These pickled eggs are merely hard-boiled eggs; the shells having been removed, they are pickled in vinegar to which fruit colorings have been added.

Plates piled high offer hot rolls, hot corn bread, plain white bread, Swedish rye, Russian rye packed with caraway seeds, Swedish twist with a garnish of poppy seeds, whole wheat bread, and the popular sweet raisin bread. Children are remembered with gingerbread men.

Several large stands are made bearing a board through which a pronged wire has been forced and left sticking out about a foot. Its prongs are eight to ten inches apart. On them are threaded big doughnuts, some plain and others sugarcoated, some coated with chocolate and others with lemon icing, while still others are glazed with plain icing.

Commonly, lemonade is put in stone jars where it is colored red, pink, or green for the children—fruit colorings being employed for this purpose. Bushel baskets of early harvest apples are placed under the trees for any hand to dip into. And every child is given a small sack containing five mints and three sticks of chewing gum. Sometimes a load of apples and a cider mill are brought to the picnic grounds and the cider drawn fresh.

Besides beverages, only one food is sold at these picnics—fried holes. These are the centers of the doughnuts which are sacked and auctioned to the highest bidder, the money raised being presented to the oldest attending settler. One might buy a very large sack, and a heavy one, paying from $.75 to $1.25 for it, only to find it contains only three or four of the little centers.

Midnight pie and coffee or hot dogs and coffee are the standard climax of Farmers' Union (Farmers' Educational and Cooperative Union) meetings in Nebraska. Sometimes several locals join for a county-wide picnic or banquet. Fried chicken is no drawing card at the outdoor affairs. Nebraska farmers get enough of that at home. Hot dogs are the never-failing favorite.

At Wisner in northeastern Nebraska, the Farmers' Union has for a number of years coupled cakes and sausage with its semiannual Dividend Day—when patronage refunds are distributed. All day long its big general store is permeated with the aroma of coffee, sizzling sausages, and frying cakes, as farm and town families "come and get 'em" along with their dividend checks.

Prizes are given to the eater of the biggest stack.

The custom of holding school picnics on the last day of school prior to the summer vacation is observed annually in many Nebraska country schools, although few town schools now follow the practice.

The potluck dinner occurs among farmers at harvest time, especially when it will work a hardship on the farmer to furnish all the food. The wives of the men working at the harvesting will make up and bring large pans of hot food. Usually there will be chicken with dumplings or fried chicken, big bowls of baked beans, stews of all kinds, vegetables of the root variety, pies, cakes, and all kinds of pickles and preserves.

In Iowa, the potluck dinner is a favorite for get-together occasions. It may be held at a family reunion, a farm picnic, an all-day quilting, a church or lodge social, or any festivity.

It is in the round of regular farming activities, in the cooperation among neighbors, that Iowa folkways appear. Many of the existing customs had their beginning in the house-raisings, huskings, hog killings, rag sewings (for carpets), quiltings, and wood-chopping bees, which filled the need for social intercourse while serving their primary purpose of cooperation in pioneer farm life. While the men worked in the fields getting the oats, wheat, barley, or rye to the threshing machine, the women gathered to cook the threshing dinners.

Some time in August or September the threshing machine comes with three or four men to attend it and a dozen or fifteen of the neigh-

Threshing near Anamosa.

bors to handle the bundles of oats, straw, and grain. The work is done in a day of high pressure. There is a strenuousness indoors as well as out, for dinner and supper have to be provided for all the hungry crowd and the threshing crew has to be kept overnight. It is the most tumultuous day of the year, but its spice of excitement lends it a certain attraction, and the work is not nearly so irksome to the men engaged as is the more solitary and sober task of corn husking that comes later.

The Iowa church-supper menu practically never varies: fried chicken or ham, mashed potatoes, gravy, stewed corn (often creamed) or green beans, coleslaw, great platters of tomatoes, bread, homemade piccalilli, jellies, coffee, and as dessert the home-baked pie—pumpkin, apple, or cherry, depending upon the season—or shortcake made in large tins and sliced. Committees of the Ladies' Aid are appointed to set the tables with salt, pepper, cream, sugar, relishes, coleslaw, and table fur-

nishings, to bring the coleslaw, to mash the potatoes which have been cooked in the church basement kitchen, to fry the chicken, to collect the tickets, and to serve extra helpings of chicken or cups of coffee.

With the passing of the log cabin and the arrival of the homesteaders, there came into Iowa the frontier festival called house-raising. At these raisings young men and boys tried their strength and skill at jumping, shooting, wrestling, and running of foot races. Black Betty— any bottle filled with Monongahela whiskey—went the rounds.

The women of the house where the festivities were to take place would be busily engaged for a day or more in preparing great quantities of food. The bread used at these frolics was baked generally on johnny- or journey-cake boards. A board was made smooth, about two feet long and eight inches wide, the ends rounded. The dough was spread out on this board and placed leaning before the fire. One side was baked, and

Threshing crew, Kessler Farm.

then the dough was changed on the board so that the other side was turned to the fire.

This became an annual festivity among farmers which persisted for three-quarters of a century. Such raisings generally took place the latter part of April, with the advent of pleasant weather.

This was in the 1840s when frame dwellings with weather-boarded walls began replacing log cabins on Iowa farms. Such houses were constructed first by laying the foundation and floor. Following this the carpenter would completely construct the four weather-boarded walls for the house while they lay flat on the ground. Invitations were then extended to some fifty or seventy-five farmers and their families for miles around to attend the raising of the walls. The farmers would accept, expecting no pay for their help. At many of these raisings there were at times more than two hundred men, women, and children.

After all the guests had assembled, which was early in the day, the men would hoist the four walls up onto the foundation and finish the

Barn-building crew, Prairieburg. Kintzle Collection.

nailing to the floors and corners. The job would be almost always completed by noon, at which time a big dinner would be served. The women of the house would be engaged for days before the event preparing food, and it was served family-style on long tables made of boards placed upon wooden horses in the dooryard.

After the dinner the floor of the new dwelling would be swept clean and dancing would begin. Music was furnished by three fiddlers and an accordion player. A hard-cider barrel was placed conveniently in the dooryard. With the advent of new methods of construction, this custom was abandoned; by 1910 it had become just another memory of the buckskin border.

Sopping in the main dish by hand was no violation of buckskin etiquette, although one etiquette book of the time indicated that "hands must not be wiped on either the tablecloth or the bread." Sopping was commonly accomplished therefore—in the better Iowa circles—by means of bread suspended on a fork, each person at the table taking a turn in describing more or less sweeping forays into the liquid sur-

Dinner on the farm, Hearst family, ca. 1933. Courtesy of James Hearst.

rounding the meat on the large platter or gravy dish and conveying it
carefully back to the mouth.

> Hello boys, ain't it a sin,
> Watch that gravy run down Sam's chin.

Whether at the table people ate what was put before them or not,
they wanted to see it there. It was part of the manner of living that the
table should indicate both the worldly status of a farmer's life and the
professional standing of his wife.

A half century and more after the last straggling remnants of free-
ranging buffalo herds were slaughtered in western Nebraska, buffalo
meat is reappearing in Nebraska on festival days.

A traveler will seldom find it on a restaurant bill-of-fare, but he may
read an invitation in the newspaper to a free helping of barbecued
buffalo at some community celebration. Once it was merely a matter of

"catching your buffalo," now it is necessary to wait until a government herd needs thinning and a few animals are being sold.

The barbecue pit is dug the previous day and a fire started in the late evening. By midnight the bottom of the pit contains a deep bed of glowing coals free from smoke. The meat is placed on the spit, and the spit must be turned at exactly the right moment to force the juices back into the roasting meat rather than letting them trickle off into the fire. The sauce, a tangy mixture of salt, pepper, vinegar, and oil, is swabbed on at intervals.

By midmorning the meat is ready to serve. A table made of boards placed across trestles is set up near the pit. Great baskets of buns, dishes of homemade pickles, and dozens of tin cups appear. The men of the village have managed the pit, but the women are taking over now. A fire is built between two flat stones, a shining new wash boiler produced, and coffee-making is under way.

Half a dozen of the village women are ranged behind the table, which boasts neither a tablecloth nor cutlery. The men have brought great platters of sliced buffalo meat, dark and a trifle stringy on the inside, crisp and dark brown around the outer edges. The hungry crowd, though giving the impression of a stampede in the beginning, has now formed an orderly line and files past the table where each is given a paper plate containing buns and several large slices of meat and has a chance to grab a pickle or two in passing. As each person secures his share of the lunch, he marches on to the steaming coffee boiler where a couple of women are ladling the hot strong brew into tin cups. There are sugar and cream for those who must have them, but the style of the day is to drink it black.

Plates and cups once filled, it is merely a matter of finding a spot of ground free of sandburs and sitting down. There is much talk and laughter, punctuated by squeals or yelps as hot coffee splashes over or concealed sandburs are discovered. The meat is nearly always tough and, despite the greatest care, has a flavor of smoke, but the sharp yet mellow sauce, combined with open-air appetites, makes second and even third helpings inevitable.

Fourth of July picnic, 1930s, Le Mars.

Sometimes a program is arranged for the afternoon. A bronco is ridden by some local champ, foot races are run, an impromptu ball game staged, or a budding orator may attempt to corral an audience. Usually, however, country women take advantage of the day in town to shop and visit with seldom-seen friends, while the menfolk congregate in groups and talk crops, herds, and politics.

But whatever else is or isn't done, the festivities end in a dance, without which no sandhill celebration is complete. Weather permitting, it is held on a platform built for that purpose near the bandstand. If the evening has turned cold, and sandhill evenings often do, a hall is usually available.

Although most people think that someone invented the popcorn ball, a Nebraska legend has it that it is actually a product of the Nebraska weather. It invented itself, so to speak, on Bergstrom Stromberg's ranch in the early days when one Febold Feboldson owned the place.

During that peculiar year known as the Year of the Striped Weather, which came between the years of the Big Rain and the Great Heat, the weather was both hot and rainy. There was a mile strip of scorching sunshine and then a mile strip of rain. It so happened that on Febold's farm there were both kinds of weather. The sun shone on his cornfield until the corn began to pop, while the rain washed the syrup out of his sugarcane.

Now the cane field was on a hill and the cornfield was in a valley. The syrup flowed down the hill into the popped corn and rolled it into great balls. Bergstrom says some of them were hundreds of feet high and looked like big tennis balls at a distance. You never see any of them now because the grasshoppers ate them all up in one day, July 21, 1874.

Old-timers who knew Febold Feboldson hold that if all the food on the table is eaten the next day will be fair.

Thick corn husks foretell a severe winter.

If a girl takes the last piece of bread on the plate she will be an old maid.

If two persons each make a wish and pull on the sides of a dried wishbone of a chicken until it breaks, the one getting the larger part will get his wish.

If two forks, knives, or spoons are accidentally put at your place at the table you will be married soon.

If a woman cuts thick slices of bread she will make a good stepmother.

If you sleep with a piece of wedding cake under your pillow your dream will come true.

The one who takes the last piece of bread or cake on the plate will remain single.

The one who takes the next to the last piece will marry a rich mate.

Peel an apple without allowing the peeling to break, hold it in your right hand over your head, circle it around you three times, and drop it over your left shoulder. The letter it forms is the initial of your future husband.

If you sit on the table you will be married before you are able.

If you take bread when you have some, someone who is hungry is coming.

If you plant potatoes on Good Friday you will have a good crop.

If you get the bubbles from your tea or coffee with your spoon before they reach the edge of the cup you will receive money.

Carrying a raw potato in one's pocket cures rheumatism.

In pioneer Nebraska schools, students and teachers brought their own noon lunches. These often consisted of cold pancakes and sow-belly. For gum, students chewed wads of white paraffin. The bread often became soggy, especially when it got mixed with such combinations as boiled turnips and dried apple pie. Often the children's lunches would freeze when carried from their homes to the schoolhouse on cold winter mornings.

The last day of school was always a gala affair, to which parents brought baskets of food for picnics after the closing exercises had taken place. The district schools were also used for box suppers, spelling bees, literaries, and in some instances sermons.

Southerners who became steamboatmen in the great inland rivers have left us today a tradition of fish frying on riverbanks and river sandbars.

To be a success, a fish fry must be held outside the confines of housed-in kitchens. Fry your fish where your picnickers can see 'em sizzle in the fat. Fish frying in a stuffy club-room kitchen is a mess at best; no matter how careful and neat one is, the odor of fish fried in deep fat will linger for weeks. A crackling wood fire and fat-filled kettles blackened by service and age have something a modern kitchen range cannot furnish. Catfish weighing from four to five pounds are most desirable.

The modern midwestern fish fry probably originated on the Middle Border when slaves were still quartered on the riverboats, along with the whites who traveled cheaply. Bunks were furnished for sleeping and a stove for cooking, but deck passengers brought aboard their own food, generally sausages, dried herring, crackers, and cheese, with whiskey to wash the dry meal down. They brought their own bedding or went without. Among these passengers were easterners who had left their rocky farms and were looking for better and cheaper land in the

Schoolgirls at picnic, Iowa City, ca. 1895–1897. Shambaugh Collection.

West, emigrants direct from Europe seeking work, and a constant stream of the restless folk to whom distant fields looked always greenest, ever moving with their reluctant wives and their brood of children, helping the crew carry wood aboard at every chance to earn a small rebate on their fare.

Up in the cabins steamboat travel was more pleasant. There was a steward to look out for the first-class travelers' needs. Under his direction meals were prepared and served and kitchen supplies bought at the landings: fruits and vegetables, lambs, pigs, and chickens. The animals were killed and dressed on board. Chickens lived until the menu called for a chicken dinner, whereupon three or four Negroes in the starboard galley, where the meats were prepared, gathered around a barrel of hot water filled from the boiler, broke the necks of the fowl over the barrel's edge, scalded, picked, and cut them—sometimes as many as 150 in an hour. The port galley where breads, cakes, pastries, and desserts were fashioned stewards kept as a showplace of cleanliness, but they usually found some excuse for not taking sight-seeing passengers to inspect the starboard galley.

Boats competed with one another in serving cabin passengers elaborate meals. On one of the packets thirteen desserts were served, six of custard, jelly, and cream in tall glasses and seven of pies, puddings, and ice cream—one each trip. Some of the northern line boats served a meal at the beginning of each run that was so heavy it was called the foundering meal and left the passengers with digestions that made them squeamish toward food for the remainder of the journey.

To the cabin passengers went this food, to those with money enough to afford the most agreeable comforts that kind of travel offered: the cotton planters from the South and Southwest, officers in government service, manufacturers, men of business, sight-seeing easterners, growers from the Middle West who had come to market their produce and were returning with large rolls of bank notes. Let the roustabouts below eat the leftovers, which the cabin passengers after every meal saw put on the deck in pans, the meats in one, the bread and cake in another, and jellies and custards in a third, followed by the cry, "Grub-pile!" To see the roustabouts rush for the broken food, grab for it, and sit down on the deck to munch on what they had managed to get their hands on! That was a spectacle to aid the digestion of the cabin passengers! To put them in good humor! "Fine weather we're havin' for this trip, sir!" "Yes, and good for the crops!" "Altogether a very satisfactory and prosperous year," they would say to one another as they sat in the shade after their meal, looking out over the broad lands that ran back from the banks of the river, and look until they were bored with looking.

The officers and crew ate together in the main cabin, the firemen at the same table with the pilots, mate, and captain. Surely in no other country under the sun could such a thing happen. The rule was that the fare should be uniform throughout. On the lower river conditions were less democratic. It was, paradoxically enough, out of the heart of

Farm garden with barn and windmill, postmarked June 23, 1913.

the South, from the great plantations, that the modern midwestern urban Negro diet was fashioned.

There were many parts of the hog that were not considered fit to eat by the people living in the Big House. So the undesirable portions of the hog, when hog-killing time came around each winter, were given to the slaves: the small intestines, called chitterlings, back bones, neck bones, feet, ears, and snouts.

> The children screamed and the children cried,
> They love groun' hog cooked and fried.

Having within them a great capacity for celebrations and having nothing to celebrate with, the slaves conceived the idea of having chitterling suppers. The intestines would be soaked and scrubbed and then soaked again. When they were considered clean enough, they were boiled for three or four hours. They are eaten as they come (from the kettle) with salt, strong black pepper, and perhaps a sauce of hot little Mexican red peppers.

Negroes developed a taste for chitterlings, which in turn created a demand for the food. The packinghouses began to prepare the hog intestines and pack them in ten- and twenty-pound pails. Saturday night chitterling suppers have become a popular form of raising money for the church and various philanthropies.

Today, in urban areas chitterlings are used more and more as sausage casings and have been taken out of the price category which originally made them accessible as a regular diet among Negroes. Pigs' tails, snouts, and all other parts that can be ground are now delicacies in the making of sausages. The only cheap meats left today are hog leg bones, which the Negroes cook with beans, peas, greens, and turnips.

Hello, Mama, make Sam quit!
He's eatin' all the hog. I can't get a bit.

After the lard was rendered, slave owners discarded the cracklings. The slaves mixed these with cornmeal and whatever flour they could get and concocted cracklin' bread. In some parts of the Middle West, cracklin' bread dinners are served at church and charity affairs.

Cracklin' dinners were more common in the past among Negroes than now. The cracklings were added to corn-bread dough and baked. The hostess and guests both furnished some of the food. These dinners were common among neighbors and friends in the winter after the hog killing and after the lard was rendered. The meal consisted of cracklin' bread, sweet milk, and fried pies. These were made of dried apples or dried peaches in a biscuit dough, shaped into triangles, and fried. They resemble filled doughnuts but are larger and made with biscuit dough.

Shortenin' bread is the progeny of "cracklin' bread." When Negroes could afford to buy lard, the melted fat was used in place of the cracklings. The other ingredients are the same. Shortenin' bread is usually fried in deep fat.

Harry Whitehead and Mose Woods, two former slaves, organized the first emancipation barbecue in Elizabethtown, Illinois, to celebrate the freeing of their people. At first, this event was attended by Negroes only. As the years went by, however, local whites joined in the festivities.

Before long, there were more whites attending the event than Negroes. The result is that the Negroes again have their own celebration. There are now two emancipation barbecues in Elizabethtown, one on the riverfront and the other in an abandoned brickyard.

If a chitterling supper is to be open to the public, it is announced a week ahead of time by a sign tacked up on a front porch giving the date and cost per plate. Besides the main dish, corn bread, coleslaw, and pickles are invariably included on the menu. Soft drinks or beer are available at an extra charge of a nickel or a dime. Included in every group are some who will not eat the chitterlings, just as there are people who will not eat sweetbreads and kidneys, but they come anyhow to enjoy the entertainment which follows the supper.

The back bones of the hog are another portion that the Big House did not consider fit to eat. These, together with neck bones, pigs' feet, ears, and tails, were passed on to the slaves. Hence their popularity with the Negro group, especially those with a trace of southern background. These are not served very often at public suppers but are more frequently the dish at social gatherings of friends and relatives during the hog-killing season. Baked back bones are generally served with sweet potatoes, corn bread, and a soft pudding made either of rice or bread and served with a plain hot sauce.

> Hello, Mama, look at Sam!
> He's eat all the hog 'n a-soppin' out the pan!

Many Nations

Many midwestern communities have large foreign elements which retain native costume and prepare foods in the Old World fashion. Nearly every community, large or small, has its Scots Society that yearly celebrates the birthday of Bobby Burns by feasting on the national dish—haggis—a mixture of oatmeal, chopped liver, and onions, alleged to be at its best when stewed in the stomach of an ox.

Favorite foods of the Cornish people, who came from Cornwall County, England, and who settled in large numbers in Michigan to become miners, are *saffern* buns and cake, meat pies made of beef, mutton, or pork, and pasties. A pastie is a mystery until you open it. It looks like a loaf of bread, but it is really a combination of boiled meat, potatoes, onions, carrots, turnips, and any other vegetable that happens to be in the house, rolled up in a sheet of dough. It is shaped like a loaf of bread, the ends folded and sealed, then baked to a delicate brown. Beef and kidney pie is also a favorite with Cornish folk.

Dobas torte hails from Romania. It is usually made of seven very thin layers of rich cake with thick, rich chocolate filling between the layers. After the layers of cake and filling are assembled, a rich chocolate frosting is put over the torte.

Germans introduced sauerkraut and wieners into Michigan as well as hasenpfeffer. The latter is rabbit parboiled in a vinegar solution. As the vinegar boils away, a tart wine is added.

Netherlanders of western Michigan have a variation on German sauerkraut using, instead of cabbage, green beans. Stores in Grand Rapids display complete lines of Dutch food, such as square bricks of black bread made from rye flour.

Young children eating watermelon, Carroll.

This bread is served at Dutch suppers, usually after a pinochle ses-
sion. After the game, the women serve the stacked bread and cold meat
and cheese, accompanied by a large bowl of potato salad and baked
beans. Usually, sliced onions, dill pickles, pretzels, and mustard follow.
Cheese may be Limburger, Swiss, Liederkranz, Camembert, Brie, or
perhaps schmierkase with schmittlach. Instead of sliced, boiled, or
baked ham, the tendency is more toward salami, chicken liver, minced
ham, tongue, pigsfoot souse, or leone sausage. Cooked meats are commonly frankfurters, wieners, Hamilton mettwurst, or bratwurst. Plenty
of beer and coffee are poured, and Dutch apple cake will top off
the meal.

Goulash was brought to Michigan as elsewhere by Hungarians. This
is a stew made of beef and veal, well seasoned with paprika. The original way of cooking goulash was to include dumplings or *spatzen*. Both
are mixtures of flour, eggs, and water dropped by the spoonful into
boiling salted water.

Russians brought appetizers to Michigan called zakuski, consisting of caviar, chopped goose liver, cold cuts of meat, and various dishes prepared with mushrooms. Sour cream is put into soup, eaten with potato pancakes, and mixed with fresh vegetables.

A Belgian booya in Michigan is a Flemish picnic. In Minnesota it is more likely to be German. The name may have been derived from an American Indian word picked up by early settlers or it may be a corruption of the French bouillabaisse. No individual picnic baskets are brought to a booya, since it is organized on cooperative lines. Large kettles of steaming chicken soup are provided, barrels of beer are set in place, and hamburgers are cooked on the grounds.

Each community has its favorite booya cook who takes pride in his skill and is always in demand. To have a woman so much as peel a potato would be unthinkable. However, women are not excluded from the feast after the cooking is finished.

At the first hint of dawn, the preparations are under way. Ox tails, a meaty soup bone, veal, and chicken—all simmer in a huge vat. The helpers are busy paring bushels of fresh vegetables, opening cans, and putting allspice in cheesecloth bags. The beans have been soaking since the previous afternoon. As soon as the meat is tender it is removed from the bones, cut in small pieces, and returned to the broth. Vegetables, cut very small, are added. When the booya is ready, the separate ingredients have lost their identity. It is neither soup nor stew nor burgoo but something of all three.

The Swedish people have introduced into Michigan a dark rye krisp, baked in thin round disks and capable of keeping for months without spoiling. This rye krisp is made of coarse rye flour, aniseed, and caraway seeds. Smorgasbord, also of Swedish origin, consists of hot and cold appetizers, pickled herring, anchovies, assorted cheeses, molded salads, and small meatballs with kidney beans. And no Swedish Christmas is complete without lutefisk. This is usually served with *julgrot*, which is rice cooked with milk. In the rice, according to a folk custom, a single nut is cooked; when the rice is served, the person who gets the nut will be the first to be married during the coming year, legend has it.

In Minnesota the lutefisk supper is a link with the immigrant past. It is also, like the reddening leaves and the flight of game birds over Minnesota's fields and lakes, a sign of fall. During the holidays, lutefisk makes at least one appearance on every good Scandinavian table, and its presence turns the meal into something like a ceremony.

Lutefisk suppers had their start in small community groups gathered for social purposes. As a symbol it provided a sentimental bond with the Scandinavian homeland. It was a token of the continuity of a beloved culture transplanted to an alien frontier. In these later days, the custom, perhaps more frequently observed now and on a wider scale, retains a measure of its former meaning. It brings folks together and reminds them of where their forefathers came from. More particularly now, it is a means of raising cash for the local church.

A plate holding two rolled napkins is placed before each person. One napkin contains a knife, fork, and spoon. Folded within the other is lefse, made of potatoes, mashed and cooled, mixed with milk and flour, rolled thin, and baked on the lids of the stove. It is served cold, which means that the women of the church can prepare it in advance on their own ranges. It looks like a piece of limp, waffled paper, cream-colored with small brown spots. To Norwegians—who will ignore the bread plate as long as a morsel of lefse remains uneaten—it has a special taste appeal. To others and to many of the youngsters, it seems rather like a tough, cold pancake with a faint potato flavor. It is to lutefisk what bacon is to eggs.

When the fall days come to Wisconsin, people in the Scandinavian areas scan their local newspapers for announcements of lutefisk suppers. Such announcements are not hard to find, because almost every Norwegian church gives at least one such supper between October and the end of the year, and there are many Norwegian churches. From miles away, often as many as fifty, lovers of lutefisk drive to the church where the supper is to be given. And they are not all Scandinavians by any means. So popular have lutefisk suppers become in Dane County that a group of Norwegians has formed a Norwegian Lutefisk Protective Association to guard the suppers from the invasion of non-Norwegian

"Unofficial Chautauqua Get-Together," with a corn roast at night, Aurelia, 1915.
Howard Preston Collection.

epicures. "Germans and Irish are again invading the sacred lutefisk domains," warns one Norwegian-American editor, "and appropriating the usual disproportionate share of the traditional Christmas delicacy." It is not uncommon for as many as two thousand people to attend a single supper, and a crowd of five hundred is considered small.

In many a Norwegian home lutefisk takes the place of the Christmas turkey. Its preparation is not complicated but takes so many days that it must be done in cold weather when the fish will not spoil. The codfish arrives already dried. Formerly it was imported from Norway where it was sun-dried, but now it is gotten from Iceland where it is electrically dried. The dry codfish is soaked in soft water for about a week—or for a longer period if the water is hard—and the water is changed each night and morning. Then the fish is removed and placed in a solution of lye and water—a gallon of soft water to two tablespoonfuls of lye—where it is soaked for another week. It is then removed from the lye solution, washed, and soaked in clean water for two days and nights. Frequently, a tablespoonful of slacked lime is added for bleaching. At the end of this time the fish is dropped into

Sewing bee on the porch, ca. 1905–1915, Clayton County.
Duluth Pieper Collection.

salted boiling water and cooked for fifteen to twenty minutes. It is served with generous sprinklings of salt, pepper, and hot melted butter. Norwegians prefer the butter sauce, Swedes a white sauce.

When church suppers are given, great quantities of fish must be prepared in advance; barrels and tubs of fish already in the lye solution are then imported from Minneapolis. Consequently, the work of the women of the church consists largely of giving the lutefisk its last soaking, boiling it, preparing the trimmings, and serving the supper.

To appear with a small appetite is the grossest kind of faux pas; to fail to stuff oneself to bursting is bad mannered. Any newcomer present will be assured, "You won't like it, nobody likes lutefisk at first. You have to learn to like it. Better take meatballs." Pitchers of melted butter are emptied lavishly on the fish and replenished time and again.

Boiled or steamed potatoes are served with it, a plain counterpoint to the fancier delicacy. Pickles are served "to take the curse off the butter." A cabbage salad, usually coleslaw, and bright dishes full of red lingonberry sauce pass up and down the tables.

When great quantities of lutefisk, boiled potatoes, and lefse have been consumed, the lutefisk-supper habitué sits back for ten or fifteen minutes, then starts all over again. At breakfast the next morning he unfolds his newspaper, glances quickly at the war news, and then scans the minor columns for an announcement of the next lutefisk supper.

The Norwegians use much of the milk that would otherwise go to waste in foods such as *rømmegrøt* and gammelost. The former is a mush made of boiled cream to which flour is added slowly, then seasoned with salt. The mush is cooked in a large iron kettle, stirred constantly, and served in bowls; sometimes it is flavored with cinnamon and sugar. Gammelost is a cheese made by heating milk which has become thick and sour until the cheese is separated from the whey. A little butter, salt, and pepper are added and the cheese placed in a crock to ferment. Weeks often pass before the proper fermenting process has taken place and the cheese is ready.

From the meat that is available on the farm the Norwegians prepare *rullpölsa*, a cold rolled meat.

The neighborliness of these people makes the coffeepot the center of kitchen activities; it is always ready on the stove, and the cupboard invariably contains a variety of pastries. In the German-Russian home it is the German coffee cake, a cinnamon-and-sugar-covered bread, rolls, and numerous cookies—all of them extremely rich. In the Norwegian home it is *Julekage*, a bread made with eggs, cream, sugar, cinnamon, raisins, and citron peel, brushed with a hot syrup, butter, and sugar; *fattigman*, a cookie made from eggs, sweet cream, and sugar and fried in deep fat; or *sandbakkels* and *berlinerkranzer*, both Norwegian cookies.

The Swedish smorgasbord, literally sandwich table, dates back to the time when people came from far-off places to attend weddings, chris-

Woman feeding chickens, rural Kensett, Worth County. Roslien Collection.

tenings, and funerals with their families and friends. Every woman brought some food, either typical of her neighborhood or something in which she excelled. While the custom of bringing food has fallen into disuse, the lavish smorgasbord survives. Restaurants feature the smorgasbord, but private homes commonly consider it too ostentatious.

A Nebraska smorgasbord menu is a varied one, consisting of about thirty dishes served buffet-style. Homemade rye bread, hard tack, white bread, coffee, pyramided butterballs, brick cheese, *kumin*, deviled eggs, cold tongue, summer sausage, liver sausage, head cheese, Swedish sausage, meatballs, pressed meat loaf, pickled herring, pickled beets, carrot slices, celery curls, radish rosettes, pickles, preserves, red apple salad. Then one comes to the hot dishes of scalloped potatoes, buttered peas, and brown beans. For dessert there is *Ost kaka* served with lingonberries and whipped cream, *trukt sappa* (fruit compote), *pepparkakor* (ginger cookies), and *sprits* (butter cookies).

For Christmas Eve dinner, stock fish is commonly served in Nebraska—a long rolled stick of dried fish prepared in Sweden or Norway. This fish is soaked for ten days in a soda solution, then in clear water, then boiled. The Swedes serve the fish with white sauce and imported lingonberries. The Norwegians serve it with butter. Christmas morning breakfast, eaten before church service, is usually a hash made from the fish, potatoes, and white sauce of the Christmas Eve dinner.

Czechs of Minnesota still raise poppies in their gardens that they may have seeds for sweet turnover rolls filled with citron which they call kolacky, and the Poles, however Americanized, still make their special cakes and wafers for religious festivals.

Nationality background affects food selection nearly as much as does locality. Thirty-five percent of the foreign stock of Nebraska is German. And wherever there are Germans there is *Eier Kuchen* (egg cake), *Deutscher Kuchen* (coffee cake), sauerkraut and *Speck* (pork), *Springalie* (Christmas cookies), pfeffernusse (cookies), and hasenpfeffer (stewed rabbit with bacon, onions, a little vinegar, and thickening).

Barbecued lamb is a traditional Serbian food. In Serbia and Montenegro the lamb is seldom slaughtered before Saint George's Day. The popular Serb belief is that it is a sin to kill such an innocent-looking animal before it matures. During the Turkish domination, which was endured nearly five centuries, Serbian guerrillas fought in much the same fashion that they fight today. During the winter months when deep snow obstructed the mountain trails, guerrillas hid with friends in the villages. But as soon as "the forests receive their dressing of green," and that is usually by Saint George's Day, the guerrillas met in the mountains for the beginning of their summer campaign. Great campfires were built and a flock of lambs slaughtered and roasted by the open fire. "The Saint George's Day when guerrillas meet" is thus an ancient saying. To get up early on that day—May 6—and meet in the forest before sunrise to lunch on cheese, barbecued lamb, and wine like the old guerrillas is an old Serb custom still observed.

Libertyville, Illinois, holds gatherings which are both Serbian and American. The tables are covered with smoked hams, roasts that smell of garlic, spinach pies (*Zeljanica*), rolled pancakes filled with fruit preserve or cottage cheese (*palatchinke*), and apple strudel. Old-timers enjoy barbecued lamb and green onions with any number of cold beers; the youngsters commonly prefer the American dishes. The parents are used to a well-organized and well-seasoned meal, but the children prefer mostly fried food, sandwiches, sweets, and cold soda water.

What one sees at Libertyville can be seen at every Serbian picnic in the Middle West. Sitting at the same table with their children and holding in their hands sizable chunks of barbecued lamb, the parents look at their American-born children in wonder and dismay, unable to understand an attachment to cold sodas and hot dogs eaten together.

The American hot dog and the Serbian barbecued lamb are old rivals, representing two worlds. The fight has been going on for decades, and it is a fight for survival. Though it is not over, judging from what we see at Serbian festivals, the barbecued lamb is waging a losing fight.

An Itoo menu, as conducted by the Lebanese of Peoria, may consist of djaaj mahshi, kebba, mihshie djaga, mihshie kussa, mihshie malfoof, loubia, and slotta.

A mass Itoo recipe to serve 2,500 calls for four hundred pounds of select beef, one hundred pounds of lamb, one hundred pounds of wheat, fifteen pounds of nuts, twelve gallons of oil, and other smaller amounts of ingredients.

The cooks begin to prepare the kebba three days in advance. They trim the beef and permit no bit of fat or rind to remain. This choice meat is then run through the grinder, inspected, and reground to compose the top and bottom layers. Then seasoning is added—onions, pepper, salt, cinnamon, kamoon, and the crushed wheat. Kamoon is a tiny, pungent, imported seed grown near Itoo on a bush similar to the one which bears aniseed. The crushed wheat is first soaked in water and drained before it is mixed with the meat.

The ground lamb filling is blended with snoubor. The snoubor is then browned in pure butter before being added to the lamb.

Approximately fifty pans, each two inches deep, fifteen inches long, and nine inches wide, are used for baking the kebba. The bottom layer is spread smooth, covered with the filling, and finished off with the top layer. The kebba is then scored into diamond shapes, drenched with oil, and baked.

Djaaj mahshi is stuffed chicken prepared in Lebanese fashion.

Mihshie kussa is another of those dishes the name of which cannot be literally translated into English. It is stuffed kussa, kussa being a peculiar vegetable shaped like a cucumber which has a distinctive flavor. Seeds for the kussa are sent or brought here from Lebanon. They are planted in the Itooans' own yards and in plots of ground in East Peoria. The kussas average twelve dozen to a bushel, each about three inches long.

Loubia is nothing more than the common green string bean dressed up. It is more or less soupy and is ladled from the bowl with a deep spoon to retain the gravy.

Eleven hundred pounds of cabbage go into the making of mihshie malfoof and there is no question but what it is especially liked by the diners. It is served with the sauce on platters.

Slotta is a juicy combination salad with a zestful flavor and a colorful appearance. It is made with head lettuce, tomatoes, parsley, green peppers, vinegar, oil, salt, and very little pepper. It is served in deep bowls.

The ingredients of the Lebanese bihlawa are so costly, the skill in preparation so exacting, and the process so lengthy that it is seldom served at public functions. The rolling process is a tedious task which requires no end of skill and patience. The dining-room table is covered with soft comforters and topped with a snowy sheet which is securely fastened to the table legs. No rolling pin is used but rather a gentle pulling motion with the hands.

Arrack, the national drink of Lebanon, means, translated, perspiration. Distilled from old grapes, it is smooth, sweet, but not thick. It is a

Picnic tables, Iowa City. Paul Juhl Collection.

liqueur comparable to the more widely known anisette. The federal government does not permit its importation, and the Lebanese here do not make enough for public distribution. So in lieu of arrack, the feast is completed with coffee and tea.

Macaroni is the basic food of South Italy and polenta that of North Italy. These, supplemented by greens, vegetables, fruit, fish, a little meat, goats' milk, cheese, eggs, bread, and wine, compose the midwestern Italian diet. Oil is the shortening used universally in the preparation of the food, though butter is used in parts, as is home-rendered lard. The elaborateness of the meals served varies with the income of the family, and a many-course dinner is as typical as a simple meal of bread, cheese, and wine.

Spaghetti is used in *pasta faggiole*, a form of macaroni served with dried peas, beans, or lentils. Spaghetti or macaroni is also used with minestrone, a thick vegetable soup or stew made with a meat stock.

In some families a dish of spaghetti may be prepared every day for the father, while the rest of the family may have something else, though they may dip into his dish. An Italian on being asked how often it is served may ask in turn, "How many days are there in the week?" To the reply, seven, he will answer, "And I eat it eight times."

On St. Joseph's Eve the table is blessed by the priest. Three people are asked by the family to represent St. Joseph, Mary, and Jesus; sometimes several children serve as angels. These and the family go to church in the morning on St. Joseph's Day. The people asked to take part in the St. Joseph feast are supposed to be poor or unfortunate; orphans are very often asked. After the church visit the group returns home, and at twelve o'clock noon the three are seated in front of St. Joseph's table and are served by some member of the family with a portion of food from every dish on the table. They must eat at least one bite of everything. What is left on their dishes is put into a bowl for them to take home. Every bit of food from the table must be eaten, since it has been blessed. Every caller to the home on St. Joseph's Day is given a portion of something from the table and a little to take home. Besides this, every visitor is served a plate of macaroni. Should any food be left after the throngs of visitors have departed, it is given to the poor.

A christening is the occasion for a large gathering of friends. Italian sandwiches, cookies, and wine are served. Singing and dancing feature the occasion. A caller who comes to see the baby is usually served with rosolio, a sweet liqueur, flavored and colored, together with Italian cookies. The refreshments most commonly served are roast beef or other meat sandwiches, Italian cookies—very often homemade—peanuts, pop, wine, and beer.

Mrs. G. Rickels baking bread in the parsonage kitchen, March 24, 1933, Atkins.
Rickels Collection.

At an Italian wedding, a long table covered with a white cloth is placed at one end of the room in front of the stage in the hall. The wedding cake, a tall affair elaborately decorated, stands in the middle and is flanked on either side by large trays of fancy cookies from the pastry shop. The bride and groom stand or are seated behind this table, and the mothers of the bride and groom are seated nearby. Placed before the bride is a bottle of rosolio, and before the groom stands a box of cigars. Each guest comes up to congratulate the bride and groom, to give them best wishes, and to present a gift, usually an envelope containing money, to the mothers who have charge of the gifts. Having received the best wishes of the guests, the bride fills a tiny glass with rosolio for the guests and invites the women to help themselves to cookies while the groom presents the men with cigars.

Among Jews, holidays are featured by special foods which it would never occur to an orthodox Jewish woman to prepare during any other time of the year.

Pesach, for example, is celebrated for a week, and during that period special china, glassware, silver, and cooking utensils are used; food eaten during that week is a reminder of the days when the Jews were slaves in Egypt. During their exodus, the Jews had only time to swing bags of flour over their shoulders as they departed. While they were in the wilderness, rain caked the flour, and the only thing they could do was to shape the mixture of flour and water into thin cakes and dry them in the sun. Today, therefore, the matzos that are eaten during Pesach are prepared out of flour and water only. Not even salt is used in the mixture. The matzos are eaten during the week of Pesach in place of bread. No flour or starch is used in the orthodox Jewish home during that week.

During the Seder bitter herbs are eaten as a reminder of the days when the lives of Jews were embittered by the hard labor that the Egyptians forced on them. Haroseth, in which the bitter herbs are dipped, is a reminder of the mixture of clay and straw out of which the Jews were forced to make bricks for their masters. Bitter herbs and haroseth are never used at any other time of the year.

On the eve of the New Year when the orthodox Jewish family gathers around the dinner table, the first food eaten is a piece of apple dipped in honey. This appetizer carries with it the hope that a sweet year is in store for all the people of the earth.

In the celebration of Purim, food takes the center of the stage. Hamantaschen are eaten only on this holiday. These small cakes are eaten all over the world by Jews. Hamantaschen symbolize the deliverance of the Jews from Haman, who had decreed that all Jews were to be killed on a certain day. Since the decree was reversed and Haman was hung for conspiracy, the hamantaschen that are eaten to commemorate his death are three-cornered cakes, since the pockets of Haman's coat were in that shape.

During Purim the Jews exchange gifts of food, a custom started when it was found that some Jews did not have the money with which to buy the ingredients for hamantaschen. To make sure that no Jew would be deprived of the joy of celebrating Purim, those Jews who could afford it supplied those who were poor. Today it is the custom to exchange gifts of food during the Purim festival.

Special dishes were created for the Sabbath, for the orthodox Jewish woman does not cook on that day. When immigration to America from Poland and Russia was at its height in the 1890s, *tscholand* was brought to America. On Friday a baking dish made out of earthenware was filled with meat, potatoes, barley, beans, and fat and sent to a public bakery and baked in a very slow oven all night. The dish was brought home in time for the noon meal. It was still hot and ready to eat.

The most popular Polish contribution to the Middle West is kielbasa, a sausage eaten cold or hot, baked, boiled, or fried. Another popular Polish dish is *khlodnik*, a cold soup made of meat and beet tops and mixed with sour cream, hard-boiled eggs, fish, and cucumbers. To this is added *kwas*, a sour liquid made by fermenting beet tops. Polish people use *kwas* to flavor dishes as the French use wine. Polish taste runs to sour food. This is even true of their soups. A soup called *barszcz* is made of thinly sliced red beets, with or without meat, to which *kwas* has been added. It is thickened with egg yolks and eaten with sour

Picnic, Jay W. Lewis and "Doc" and their families, Coffin Grove,
Delaware County, ca. 1905.

cream. Poles often prefer meat sour; pot roast is thus marinated in
boiled vinegar before it is cooked.

On Holy Saturday—the day before Easter Sunday—the mother of
the family sends one of her children to church with a basket of food to
be blessed. The basket may contain kielbasa, butter rolls fashioned in
the form of lambs, colored eggs, a little vinegar, salt, pepper, and
horseradish. On Easter morning every member of the family partakes
of the food, each thereby being blessed.

The day following Easter is sometimes observed as *Dyngus Day*, or
Switching Day. On this occasion the children beat their sisters, aunts,
and female relations lightly with small switches about the legs. The
child then receives a penny, a colored egg, or a nut in exchange for the
switch.

Nine meatless courses customarily accompany the celebration of
Christmas in a Polish home. Courses commonly include herring (*sled-*

zie), perch (*okonki*), halibut (*biala ryba*), oysters (*slimski*), cheese dumplings (*pierogi*), potato dumplings (*kartoflane kluski*), egg pancakes (*placki na jajkach*), sauerkraut with mushrooms (*kapusta z grzybami*), crullers (*kruscziki*), Christmas cookies (*pierniki*), mushroom soup (*grzybowa zupa*), and meatless borsch (*postny borsch*).

In the center of the table on this occasion are wafers (*oplatki*) obtained by the mother from the church after being blessed there. Each member of the family receives one of these and shares it with the others while wishing them health, wealth, and happiness. A blessing is then said, and the meal is eaten.

It is felt that by depriving oneself of meat on these occasions atonement for sin is achieved. A little food is left on each plate in order that in the year to come one may not want for food.

Bohemians of the Nebraska mudhills serve kolacky, a kind of biscuit dough pressed down in the center with prunes or apricots and sprinkled with poppy seeds and baked. *Rohliky* is made of kolacky dough kneaded and twisted into the shape of a half-moon and sprinkled with poppy seeds. Their rye bread has caraway seeds in it. These baked foods are served at the Sokol. Other foods served there are potato dumplings with sauerkraut, roast chicken, gravy, baked pork, peas, corn, baked beans, coleslaw made with cucumbers and cream, pie, cake, and coffee. The pies are usually apple, peach, or pumpkin. Jell-O is served more frequently than ice cream. Keg beer is always served.

The Bohemian women enjoy feather-stripping bees and quilting bees. At the former they meet in a kitchen and strip the feathers for feather beds and pillows. As they work they visit and gossip, while the men sit in the front room and play cards. The lunch served on both occasions always includes kolacky and coffee. Wieners, chicken, mock chicken, or ham is served on buns. Cake or cookies are served more often than pie. Sometimes strudel is served.

Foods similar to those served at the feather-stripping bees or the Sokol picnics may be served at church or lodge suppers.

A dish frequently served in Bohemian homes is the potato pancake,

Quilting bee at the home of Jessie W. Anderson, North Liberty, January 1951.
Jessie White Anderson Collection.

which is a potato dumpling baked on the top of the stove. Some Bohemians bake bread in the oven without a pan. Bohemian women sometimes bring to picnics a dish popular with both Bohemians and Germans. Long thin strips of fat bacon or salt pork slightly seared are dusted with bread crumbs; on this, thin layers of parboiled liver are spread; over these meat layers, more bread crumbs, sliced red and green peppers, finely chopped rutabagas; and these are covered with large cabbage leaves. The whole is then rolled and tied with a string. This roll is threaded onto a clean stick and the whole cooked and served hot or cold by slicing crosswise. During the cooking process, thyme and bay leaves are used.

The country kitchen, whether in the Nebraska sandhills or on the plains of Ohio, was a workshop for converting raw materials into hu-

Gabelmann sisters butchering ducks, Clarksville.

man food. Poultry bought alive had to be picked and drawn there. Cabbage for coleslaw was hand-chopped in wooden bowls. Beans were soaked overnight to soften. Steaks were pounded with a mallet. There was no such thing as quick-rising baking powder, and biscuits had to be set with saleratus and vinegar, while coffee, bought green in the berry, was roasted and ground in a hand-turned grinder, through which was run cornmeal to remove the taste if it had been previously used for grinding pepper.

Nebraska Danes eat veal rolled up and cooked in spiced water, chilled, and sliced and call it *Rolla Pailse*. Another Danish favorite is a liver loaf made from ground raw liver, ground salt pork, spices, and eggs, all of which is put in a loaf pan lined with cheesecloth. It is steamed an hour, baked an hour, then chilled and sliced.

Milk, cream, and butter form a substantial part of the Danish diet. They use only butter as a shortening for pastry. *Danske Kage* and

Bakery interior, Amana bakery, Homestead.

Wienerbrod are among the more popular cakes. The Danes eat a great deal of clabbered milk, a soup made from buttermilk, rice, and flour, boiled until thick and flavored with sugar and lemon peel. Sometimes raisins are added, and the mixture is topped off with whipped cream. A soup made of barley and apples, flavored with raspberry juice or jelly, is also popular. Cream gravies and sauces and sour cream dressings are favorites among the Danes. In fact, there are very few recipes that do not call for milk or cream. Desserts are always very rich with thick cream. Cheese is a daily food, and in many Danish homes the cheese dish is always on the table.

Everyone brings *Kött Bulla*—little round meatballs—to the Swedish midsummer festival. There is always the *Liebkuchen*, or sweet bread, or cookies for the special benefit of the children, who never seem to get enough of them, for these little square cookies contain eggs, sugar, honey or syrup, pecan meats, spices, currants, chocolate, citron, milk, baking powder, and flour.

Baking bread, Homestead.

Most of the Russians of Nebraska are German-Russians who moved to Russia from Germany and from there to Nebraska and the Dakotas. Now the Russian families in Lincoln are really Russian. Some of their favorite dishes:

Krautranze:
   Cabbage and meat rolled in wheat-flour dough and baked.
Haevaglaze:
   Made of wheat-flour dough only and in a kettle with pork or beef.
Glaze:
   Mixture of cubed potatoes seasoned, rolled in wheat-flour dough, and fried.
Grebell:
   A dough made of wheat flour only, fried in cooking oil; sort of a doughnut.

Rawnze:
Cherries or apples spread on a piece of dough, the four corners of the dough folded together, and baked.
Pigs in a blanket:
Meatballs rolled in a leaf cabbage and boiled.

Probably at very few places will one find bread baked as at the Amana Colonies in Iowa, where for over eighty years it has been kneaded by hand and baked on a heated oven floor. The baker heats the oven with pieces of wood, the number of which he has counted. After the pieces have finished burning and there is no fire under the oven, the bread is put in to bake. The loaves—about one hundred—are removed by long-handled wooden paddles about the length of canoe paddles or longer. Scarcely a visitor leaves the villages without taking along a crusty two-pound loaf of hearth-baked bread.

Two Welsh contributions to the Iowa diet are the seed cake and froise, a griddle tea cake commonly preferred on St. David's Day when the evening is occupied by auctioning or raffling a quilt made community style by the Welsh ladies. The balance of the occasion is rounded out with the old dances that give way to the more modern as the evening progresses and the youths take up the more recent steps in swingtime.

Froise was usually eaten at the afternoon tea meal in Wales. It is a dish that can be served anytime a light food is desirable—breakfast, lunch, dinner, or supper.

These are the foods of many nations, brought from many lands to nourish one land. They are all the Old World ways which have gone into the great melting pot of the Middle West, to come out behind the counter of the all-night hamburger stand on U.S. 66 or in the quick-service businessman's lunch on any downtown street in Minneapolis, Akron, or Omaha. These are the blue plate specials, the streamlined steaks, and the laborer's lunch pail, passed down an endless boardinghouse table from a brave in buckskin to a blue-turbaned voyageur, from a coonskin Yankee to a drawling steamboatman, from a Negro fish-vendor to an Irish section hand.

Many foods, many nations. Yet one food, one nation. Many lands, one land.

Foods of Many Folk

APPLE PIE
Old Time / American

―――――

1 cup dried apples
½ cup brown sugar
½ teaspoon ground cinnamon
½ teaspoon nutmeg
¼ teaspoon salt
pie crust

Soak apples in water to cover, overnight. Remove all cores and boil with the brown sugar and spices. Put a large spoonful of the apple mixture on a square of pie crust, cover with another square, and pinch together. Fry in deep fat until brown. Sprinkle with powdered sugar as they are taken from fat.

BERENJENAS RELLENAS
Stuffed Eggplant / Spanish

―――――

1 eggplant
1 onion
1 tomato
1 cup cooked chicken
olive oil or butter
salt and pepper

Cut the eggplant lengthwise and blanch in boiling water for 10 minutes. Remove the pulp from it, being careful not to break the skins. Chop the onion, tomato, and chicken, and cook in a little olive oil or butter. Add about half of the eggplant pulp. Season with salt and pepper and mix well. Stuff the eggplant and bake in medium oven about 15 minutes.

BLINIS
Russian Pancakes

————

1 ounce yeast
3 cups warm milk
¾ pound buckwheat flour
3 eggs
½ teaspoon salt
½ cup butter

Dissolve the yeast in 1 cup of warm milk and mix in a little of the flour. Let stand in a warm place for 2 hours. Then add the rest of the flour, the yolks of the eggs, salt, and the rest of the warm milk. Mix well but do not let batter get too thick. Beat the whites of the eggs until stiff and add, mixing well. Let stand for another half hour. Fry in butter in a very small frying pan. Serve with caviar or sour cream.

BLINTZES
Cheese Pancakes / Jewish

————

BATTER
1 cup milk
4 eggs
1 teaspoon salt
1 cup flour

FILLING

1½ pounds cottage cheese
2 eggs
1 tablespoon melted butter
3 tablespoons sugar

Batter: Add the milk to the well-beaten eggs and salt. Stir in the flour gradually; mix until batter is smooth. Heat a 6-inch spider, grease with a little vegetable fat, and pour 2 tablespoons evenly over the bottom of the spider. When the pancake begins to blister, it is done. Turn out on a flat surface, brown-side up.

Filling: Put cheese through ricer. Add the eggs, melted butter, and sugar and mix well. Put a tablespoon of the cheese on each pancake and fold over like an envelope. Fry in butter on both sides, until a golden brown. Serve with sour cream or sugar and cinnamon.

BOOYA
60 Gallons / Flemish

———

30 pounds ox tails
10 pounds beef soupbones
4 fat hens
½ bushel tomatoes (or 2 gallons puree)
1 peck onions
1 peck carrots
1 peck potatoes
1 peck kohlrabi
6 heads cabbage
12 stalks celery
6 cans corn
6 cans peas
2 quarts navy beans, soaked in cold water 12 hours
2 quarts string beans

1 peck barley
1 10-cent can allspice (put in a bag)
1½ ounces paprika
3 pounds salt
pepper to taste

Boil the meat in water to cover, until tender. Remove meat from bones and cut into small pieces. Add all vegetables diced, add spices, and cook until done. Always keep enough water to cover.

BREAKFAST SCONES
English

———

2 tablespoons butter
1 cup flour
½ teaspoon baking soda
½ teaspoon cream of tartar
pinch of salt
1 egg
enough milk to make a light dough

Rub the butter into the flour. Add soda, cream of tartar, and salt. Then the egg well beaten and the milk. Roll out on floured board and cut into rounds. Bake in a quick oven.

BRUNOISE
Vegetable Soup / French

———

2 large carrots
1 large onion
1 small leek
1 stalk celery
3 tablespoons peas

3 tablespoons cut string beans
2 tablespoons butter
4 cups hot water
salt and pepper to taste

Cut all the vegetables in small pieces. Melt the butter in a saucepan and put in the vegetables (except the peas). Simmer slowly in the butter till the vegetables are brown. Add the hot water, salt, and pepper and cook 1 hour. Add the peas and cook half an hour longer.

BURGOO
Modern Recipe / Armenian

———

1 5-pound chicken
1 2-pound beef shank
1 gallon water
4 ears of corn
6 tomatoes
12 potatoes
3 onions
salt to taste

The chicken and the beef shank are cut up and put into a large kettle with the water. When the meat is almost done, add the vegetables diced. The corn is cut from the cobs. Cook until all vegetables are done. Salt to taste. This dish needs constant stirring to prevent scorching.

CHARCHOUKA
African

———

5 large onions
3 tablespoons olive oil
5 large tomatoes

3 pimientos
1 small hot pepper
1 teaspoon salt
4 eggs

Cut the onions into small pieces and brown in the oil. Peel and slice the tomatoes and add when onions are a golden brown. Simmer for 5 minutes, then add the pimientos and hot pepper, cut into tiny pieces, and the salt. Simmer until all the vegetables are reduced to a pulp. Pour into 4 individual casseroles and drop an egg into each. Bake until egg is set.

CHICKEN CHEESE
American

———

1 4-pound chicken
1 onion
1 stalk celery
1 carrot
salt to taste

Boil chicken and vegetables until tender. Remove from broth and boil broth down till there is about 1 cup left. Cut the meat from the chicken and chop it. Put the vegetables through a sieve. Put all into a mold and pour the broth over it. Salt to taste. Put in refrigerator to harden. Unmold and slice. Garnish with hard-boiled sliced eggs, if desired.

EGG BREAD
Southern American

———

½ pint white cornmeal
1 tablespoon melted lard
3 eggs
⅔ cup sweet milk

⅔ *cup sour milk*
¼ *teaspoon salt*

Mix all ingredients thoroughly and bake in a well-greased, heated shallow pan.

F R O I S E
Welsh

————

4 eggs
1 teaspoon salt
1 teaspoon baking powder
enough flour to make a thin batter
dried currants

Beat the eggs and add salt and baking powder. Stir in the flour. Grease a griddle and pour in the batter, sprinkle with the currants and turn over and brown on the other side. Spread with butter and sugar.

G O U L A S H   A N D   S P A E T Z L E
Beef and Veal Stew / Hungarian

————

1 onion
3 tablespoons fat
1 #2 can of tomatoes
1 pound beef cut in small pieces
salt and pepper
1 pound veal cut in small pieces
1 teaspoon paprika
1 egg
½ cup water
1½ cups flour

Cut the onion into small pieces and brown in the fat. Add the tomatoes and bring to a boil. Season beef with salt and pepper and add to tomatoes. Simmer for about 1½ hours, then add the veal seasoned with salt. Simmer another hour.

Beat the egg; add salt and water and stir into the flour until a smooth batter is formed. Drop by tablespoons into a large kettle of boiling salted water. Boil until they rise to the top, then simmer slowly 5 minutes longer. Drain in colander and serve with the goulash.

GRAPE WINE
For Passover / Jewish

———

4 12-pound baskets concord grapes
11 pounds sugar
2 quarts water

Wash grapes and pick from stems. Put them in a large crock with 1 pound of sugar. Cover with a cheesecloth and let stand for 1 week. Then press grapes through fruit press. Boil the 10 pounds of sugar with 2 quarts of water. Add to grape juice. Put into 5-gallon keg. Keep keg filled so that the wine can work and overflow. After it stops working, put in bung with vent. Change to tight bung a month later.

HACKAD BIFF MED LOK
Minced Beef with Onions / Swedish

———

2 pounds chopped beef
salt and pepper
2 tablespoons butter
1 onion

Season the meat with salt and pepper and shape into cakes. Fry them in the melted butter, about 1 minute on each side. Slice onion and fry until golden brown and put over the meat cakes. Add about half a cup of hot water and bake about 30 minutes. Serve hot.

HAMANTASCHEN
Poppy Seed Cakes / Jewish

———

1 pound black poppy seeds
1 cup milk
1 cup honey
1 cup raisins
½ cup chopped nuts
coffee cake dough

Grind the poppy seeds in a poppy seed grinder. Boil in the milk for 5 minutes. Add the other ingredients and mix well. Roll the dough into a sheet about half an inch thick and cut into 4-inch squares. On each square put a tablespoon of the poppy seed mixture and pinch into a three-cornered cake. Brush with honey and bake in a medium oven.

HARVEST HOME DRINK
American

———

10 gallons cold water
1 gallon molasses
1 quart vinegar
¼ pound ground ginger

Mix all together and serve cold.

LE HOCHEPOT
Hotchpotch / Belgian

———

2 pounds brisket of beef
2 pounds shoulder and breast of mutton
2 pounds shoulder of veal
2 pounds pigs' feet
¾ pound pigs' ears
½ pound pigs' tails
salt and pepper
1 large head cabbage
2 carrots
4 leeks
4 stalks celery
12 pickling onions
mixed spices

Season all the meat with salt and pepper and put into kettle. Cover with cold water and bring to boiling point. Skim well until the scum has stopped rising. Then add the vegetables sliced and seasoned with salt. Put the spices in a bag and add. When all the meat is tender, it is arranged on a platter, and the soup is served as a separate course.

LUKEFISK
Minced Fish / Norwegian

———

5 tablespoons butter
½ cup flour
1½ cups hot milk
salt and pepper
nutmeg
1 cup boiled minced fish
1 cup diced boiled potatoes

Melt the butter in a saucepan and mix in the flour without browning. Add the milk slowly and stir constantly until thick. Season with salt, pepper, and nutmeg to taste. Add the fish and potatoes and cook 5 minutes.

MEXICAN RICE
Mexican

———

1 cup rice
2 tablespoons butter
1 cup strained tomatoes
2 teaspoons salt
1 quart boiling water

Wash rice and dry. Melt butter in spider and put in the rice. Let fry until light brown, stirring constantly. Add tomatoes and salt and simmer 5 minutes. Add boiling water, stir well, and cook until rice is tender.

OLLEBROD
Beer Bread / Danish

———

10 ounces rye bread
½ cup water
2 pint bottles pale ale
sugar
grated rind of ½ lemon
cream

Cut the bread into small pieces and soak in the water and 1 bottle of ale for 12 hours. Put in a saucepan and simmer for 20 minutes. Rub through a sieve and put back into saucepan. Add the other bottle of ale and bring to boiling point. Add sugar to taste and the lemon rind. Boil a few minutes longer and serve with cream.

POLENTA
Yellow Cornmeal Mush / Italian

———

1 cup yellow cornmeal
4 cups boiling water
1 teaspoon salt

Stir the cornmeal into the boiling salted water. Cook until mush is thick. Pour into shallow pan and allow to cool and harden.

SAUCE FOR POLENTA
2 kidneys
1 onion
1 tablespoon butter
1 tablespoon lard
salt
1 cup water
1 tablespoon flour

Cut the kidneys in pieces and parboil for about half an hour. Brown the onion, which has been ground, in the butter and lard. Add the kidneys, season with salt. Add the water and thicken with the flour. Pour over slices of polenta.

PROSIAK FASZEROWANY
Stuffed Suckling Pig / Polish

———

1 pig not over 6 weeks old
2 onions
¾ cup butter
2 goose livers
½ pound mushrooms
1 tablespoon parsley
2 eggs

½ teaspoon dill
marjoram to taste
tarragon to taste
salt and pepper to taste

Brown the minced onions in the butter. Chop all the ingredients and add to browned onions. Add the eggs and mix well. Stuff the pig and sew it up. Roast for 1 or 2 hours, until tender.

PUDIM DE NOSES
Walnut Pudding / Portuguese

———

½ pound walnuts
3 eggs
1 cup sugar
½ teaspoon cinnamon

Shell the walnuts and pound them in a mortar to a paste. Beat the eggs, add the sugar, and mix well. Add the nuts and cinnamon and mix again. Butter a pudding mold and turn in the mixture. Put the mold in a pan of boiling water and bake until set.

SEED CAKE
Welsh

———

½ cake yeast
½ cup lukewarm water
½ cup shortening
1 cup sugar
1 teaspoon salt
1 teaspoon caraway seed
2 eggs
2 cups flour

Dissolve the yeast in the lukewarm water and mix with the rest of the ingredients. Mix well and place in a buttered cake mold. Let rise to double size and bake about 1 hour.

SOUPA AVGHOLEMONO
Lemon Soup / Greek

―――――

1 tablespoon rice
1 quart chicken soup
2 egg yolks
1½ lemons

Boil the rice in the chicken soup until the rice is tender. Mix the yolks with a little warm water and stir with the juice of the lemons. Serve as soon as ready.

SPAGHETTI SAUCE
Italian

―――――

1 large onion
1 clove of garlic
¼ cup olive oil
1 can pomidoro pasto
½ cup water
1 green pepper
1 pimiento

Mince the onion and the garlic and cook slowly in the oil. Onion should be cooked thoroughly but not browned. Add the pomidoro pasto, the water, and the green pepper and pimiento, cut in tiny pieces. Cook 5 minutes longer. Add the water and cook 1 hour. Serve with boiled spaghetti.

STOKVISCH
Stock Fish / Dutch

———

1 pound dried codfish
mustard sauce

Soak the codfish in cold water for 12 hours. Skin and bone and cut into slices. Roll each slice and tie with a string. Boil in salted water for 1 hour. Remove string and serve with baked onions and rice and mustard sauce.

TADJIN AHMAR
Mutton Stew with Prunes / Arabian

———

½ pound prunes
4 pounds mutton from the neck
salt
olive oil
1 onion
1 cup boiling water
1 stick cinnamon
pinch of saffron
2 tablespoons sugar

Soak the prunes in cold water overnight. Cut the mutton into 2-inch strips and season with salt. Brown the meat in a little olive oil. When the mutton is brown, put it into casserole and add the onion, minced, the boiling water, the stick of cinnamon, and the saffron, which has been softened in a little hot water. Mix well and bake about 2 hours. Add prunes and sugar and bake another hour. Serve in casserole.

TIN SUIN PAI KWE
Pork with Sweet-Sour Sauce / Chinese

---

2 cloves garlic
2 teacups vinegar
¼ cup sugar
Chinese sauce
corn flour water
salt and pepper
1½ pounds pork cutlets
¼ cup flour
2 eggs
½ pound mixed pickles

Prepare the sweet-sour sauce first. Sprinkle a little salt into an oiled frying pan. Crush the garlic with a knife and cook for a second. Remove garlic, put in the vinegar, sugar, a drop of Chinese sauce, about a teaspoon corn flour water, and a speck of pepper.

Season the meat with salt and pepper and coat with the flour. Beat the eggs and dip the meat in the eggs. Cook in hot oil for 15 minutes. Remove from the oil and drain. Bring the sweet-sour sauce to a boil and put the meat and the mixed pickles into it. Stir for 1 minute and serve.

WIENER SCHNITZEL
Vienna Veal Steak / Austrian

---

4 thin slices veal
salt and pepper
2 tablespoons flour
1 egg
white bread crumbs
3 tablespoons fat

Sprinkle the veal with salt and pepper. Dip each slice in the flour, then in the well-beaten egg, then in the bread crumbs. Fry in the hot fat until light brown. Finish baking in the oven about half an hour. Serve with lemon.

ZABAGLIONE
Italian

———

3 egg yolks
1½ tablespoons sugar
just over ½ cup sherry
1 teaspoon lemon juice

Beat yolks and sugar till fluffy. Add sherry and lemon juice. Mix well. Pour into double boiler. Stir with egg beater over fire. Do not boil. When starts to rise, pour into glasses. Serve hot. Makes 2 portions.

Tested & Rewritten Recipes

APPLE PIE
Old Time / American

------

5 medium Granny Smith apples, pared, cored, and sliced
½ cup light brown sugar
¼ teaspoon ground cinnamon
¼ teaspoon nutmeg
¼ teaspoon salt
3 tablespoons water
2 tablespoons butter
1 2-crust pie dough (we used Pillsbury's frozen)
fat for frying (optional)
powdered sugar for sprinkling

1. In a small bowl, sprinkle apples with sugar, cinnamon, nutmeg, and salt; add 3 tablespoons water and toss.
2. In heavy fry pan over medium heat, melt butter and add apple mixture, scraping the inside of the bowl with rubber spatula. Cover pan with tight-fitting lid and simmer for 15 to 20 minutes, turning occasionally.
3. Remove lid and increase heat to evaporate liquid. Let the filling cool to room temperature. (This can be done a day ahead and refrigerated.)
4. Follow package directions for pie crust or make your own pie dough.

5   Place bottom crust in a pie pan, transfer filling to the pie crust, cover with second crust, and cut hole in the middle. Pinch the edges of top and bottom crusts together and bake according to package directions.

Note:

To make the individual fried pies as the original recipe suggests, divide each pie crust into 6 wedges and spoon out the filling so you can fold half of each wedge over the other half. Press edges and place on lightly buttered cookie sheet. Bake 15 to 20 minutes less than for whole pie.

If you insist on "authenticity," fry the individual pie wedges in deep fat at a fairly high temperature, turning once if necessary. Place on paper towel, sprinkle with powdered sugar, and serve warm.

We also made the pie from pie-dough sticks, following the package directions, rolling the dough into a rectangular sheet, and cutting it into 12 4-by-4-inch squares. Divide the filling on the left side of the squares, fold the other half over, press the three sides with fork tines, and then deep fry. We had the best results using a 50:50 peanut oil and lard mixture. Because of the high smoking point, the pies absorbed the least fat.

BERENJENAS RELLENAS
Stuffed Eggplant / Spanish

––––––

1 eggplant (approximately 16 to 20 ounces or
2 smaller ones totaling 22 to 26 ounces)
water to cover
1 tablespoon salt
3 tablespoons olive oil or butter, or combined
½ cup chopped onion
2 cups pared, chopped tomatoes (approximately 3 to 4 firm ripe tomatoes)
2 cups (approximately) chopped, precooked eggplant

1 teaspoon sugar
1 teaspoon salt
¼ teaspoon black pepper
1 cup cooked and cubed chicken

Preheat oven to 350 degrees.

1   Cut the eggplant, with the stem, lengthwise and blanch in boiling salted water for 10 minutes. Remove and rinse with cold water to cool.

2   With sharp knife and spoon, remove the pulp, leaving about a ½ inch. Be careful not to break the skin. Place skins, cavity up, in an oven-proof dish.

3   Put olive oil or butter in frying pan, add the onion, and cook until slightly brown. Add tomatoes, chopped eggplant, sugar, salt, pepper, and slowly cook. Add chicken, heating it through. Place mixture in the skins and bake in preheated oven 15 to 20 minutes.

4   Serve as is or with ketchup or with sauce made from adding 2 or 3 dashes of Tabasco sauce, pinch of salt, and 1 teaspoon of an aromatic herb (such as basil, dill, parsley, or cilantro) to 1 cup sour cream or plain yogurt. Offer fluffy white rice as a side dish.

BLINIS
Russian Pancakes

———

1 ounce yeast (active yeast in cake form preferred)
1 cup warm milk
1 teaspoon sugar
1½ cups buckwheat flour
3 medium eggs, separated
½ teaspoon salt
2½ cups warm whole milk
caviar
sour cream

1   Dissolve yeast in 1 cup of warm milk and mix in sugar and 3 table-
     spoons of the flour. Let stand in warm place for 2 hours.
2   Add the rest of the flour, egg yolks beaten slightly with a fork, salt,
     and the rest of the warm milk. Mix well but do not let batter get too
     thick.
3   Beat egg whites until stiff and add, mixing well. Let stand for an-
     other ½ hour.
4   Fry singly in butter in very small frying pan or 3 or 4 at a time in a
     regular-size pan. If you fry 2½-inch pancakes, this batter will yield
     approximately 45 pancakes.
5   Serve with caviar or sour cream or both.
6   Offer chopped hard-boiled egg yolks, egg whites, and chopped
     onions with it.

Note:

You may prebake blinis several hours or a day ahead, then pack in
aluminum foil and heat in a medium oven for 10 to 15 minutes. Do not
bake too high. If intended for freezing, put 2 sheets of foil between each
layer for quick and easy defrosting. May be kept frozen for about a
month. Do not freeze the batter, but it can be refrigerated overnight.

BLINTZES

Cheese Pancakes / Jewish

———

BATTER

1 cup milk
4 large eggs
1 teaspoon salt
1 cup flour
shortening for frying

FILLING

1½ pounds baker's cheese, dry cottage cheese, or small-curd cottage cheese
2 large eggs
1 tablespoon melted butter

½ cup sugar
sour cream and cinnamon sugar or sweetened low-fat yogurt

Batter:

Add milk to well-beaten eggs and salt. Stir in flour gradually; mix until batter is smooth. Heat a 6-inch spider or heavy 6-inch frying pan, brush with oil, and pour 2 tablespoons of batter evenly over bottom of pan, tilting pan left and right so batter runs evenly. When it begins to blister, the pancake is done. Turn out with a spatula, brown side up.

Filling:

1   Put cheese through strainer or ricer.

2   Add eggs one by one after beating vigorously with fork; add the melted butter and sugar; mix well. Place heaping tablespoon of cheese on each pancake and fold over. Repeat until all ingredients are used.

3   Place in an oven-proof, preferably glass dish. Before serving, fry the blintzes on both sides with a little butter or butter and oil mixed until brown; return them to oven-proof dish and keep in oven at 200 to 250 degrees until serving. If you prefer not to fry, place blintzes in oven-proof dish and heat at 300 to 325 degrees for 20 to 25 minutes. Top with sour cream and cinnamon sugar or sweetened low-fat yogurt.

BOOYA
8 Gallons / Flemish

———

3 pounds ox tails (cut into 1-inch-thick disks, trimmed)
2 pounds beef soup bones (cut into small pieces)
1 stewing hen, approximately 4 pounds (cut into quarters)
1 can (12 ounces) tomato puree
2 cups chopped onion
2 cups chopped carrots

3 cups chopped potatoes
2 cups chopped kohlrabi (or turnip)
½ head cabbage, chopped
2 stalks celery, chopped
12 ounces frozen corn
12 ounces frozen peas
1 pound canned navy beans
1 12-ounce box frozen string beans
1 cup barley
½ teaspoon ground allspice
1 tablespoon paprika
1½ cups salt
3 teaspoons freshly ground black pepper

Boil meat in water to cover, until tender. Remove meat from bones and cut into small pieces. Readjust water level to 8 gallons. Add rest of ingredients, divide among 2 5-gallon pots, and cook in preheated 350-degree oven approximately 3 hours. Maintain the water level to cover (about 8 gallons).

Note:

The recipe in Algren's manuscript is for 60 gallons. We reduced it to approximately 8 gallons and it was excellent. It makes a great party dish. Its great advantage is that it can be prepared in 2 5-gallon soup pots and finished in the oven without watching. This recipe uses more vegetables than all the other recipes put together.

BREAKFAST SCONES
English

———

½ teaspoon baking soda
½ teaspoon cream of tartar
pinch of salt

1 cup flour
2 tablespoons butter
1 egg
enough milk to make a light dough

Preheat oven to 400 degrees.
1   Add baking soda, cream of tartar, and salt to flour. Sift together.
2   Rub butter into flour mixture.
3   Add egg, well beaten with fork, and the milk, not more than 2 tablespoons to start with, then a little more if needed.
4   Roll out on floured board and cut into 8 rounds.
5   Bake in a quick oven at 400 degrees for 12 to 15 minutes.
    Yield: 8 scones.

BRUNOISE
Vegetable Soup / French

———

2 cups chopped carrots
1½ cups chopped onion
1 small leek (approximately 1 cup chopped, white part only)
½ cup celery, chopped
3 tablespoons cut string beans
2 tablespoons butter
4 cups hot water plus 1 teaspoon Minor's chicken base or vegetable base
salt and pepper to taste
3 tablespoons peas

1   Cut all vegetables in small pieces.
2   Melt butter in saucepan and add vegetables (except peas). Cover, simmer slowly until vegetables are brown, add hot water, soup base, salt and pepper, and cook 1 hour.
3   Add peas and cook 10 minutes.

Note:

Freshly picked vegetables versus those purchased in a store can produce varying results. When testing the recipes, the addition of the soup bases made a remarkably favorable difference. Minor's soup bases are available nationwide through mail order. For a catalog call 1-800-441-9514, L. J. Minor, 30003 Bainbridge Road, Solon, OH 44139.

BURGOO
Modern Recipe / Armenian

----

1 4- to 5-pound chicken
1 2-pound beef shank
1 gallon water
½ cup salt (plus more to taste)
4 ears fresh corn, approximately 3 cups cut up
6 tomatoes, approximately 1 quart cubed
1 quart potatoes, peeled and cubed
3 cups chopped onions

1   Cut up chicken and beef. Place in large kettle with the water and salt. Bring to a boil, then simmer over medium heat, covered, until meat is almost done.

2   Remove meat, let it cool enough to handle, cut into bite size. Discard bones and chicken skin, skim fat from top of broth. Place the raw vegetables in large oven-roasting pan (with cover). Add meat, pour on liquid, add some fresh ground black pepper and garlic salt. Adjust volume of liquid to 1 gallon, cover and bake for 1½ to 2 hours at 350 degrees. Serve hot. All vegetables will retain their color, texture, and taste, and you don't have to watch the pot.

CHARCHOUKA
African

———

3 cups sliced onions
3 tablespoons olive oil or corn oil
5 large tomatoes, firm but red, peeled and cubed
1 tablespoon sugar
2 large red peppers, cut into tiny pieces
1 small hot pepper, jalapeño or similar, according to taste,
cut into tiny pieces
1 teaspooon salt
4 eggs

Preheat oven to 350 degrees.

1   Slice onions, brown in oil over high heat. Keep stirring.
2   Peel and cube the tomatoes and add when onions are golden brown.
    Add sugar. Simmer 5 minutes, then add red and hot peppers cut into
    tiny pieces, and the salt. Simmer covered over medium heat until
    all vegetables are reduced to a pulp (20 to 30 minutes).
3   Pour into 4 individual casseroles and drop egg into each. Bake until
    egg is set, 5 to 6 minutes.
4   Offer Tabasco or an African hot sauce on the side.

CHICKEN CHEESE
American

———

1 4-pound chicken
1 onion, peeled and cut in half
1 carrot, scraped and cut into 4 pieces
1 stalk celery, cut into 4 pieces
salt to taste (we used 1 tablespoon)
2 to 3 tablespoons lemon juice or 1 to 2 tablespoons vinegar (optional)
hard-boiled, sliced eggs for garnish (optional)

1   Cut chicken in 4 quarters, peel and cut onion in half, scrape carrot, cut up with celery.
2   Boil chicken and vegetables in water to barely cover with 1 table-spoon salt until tender, then remove. Boil broth down to about 2 cups.
3   Cut meat from the chicken and chop. Discard skin or chop very fine.
4   Put the vegetables through a sieve, colander, or ricer.
5   Place in a mold and pour the broth over it. Mix. Add lemon juice or vinegar. Refrigerate to harden. Unmold and slice.
6   Garnish with hard-boiled, sliced eggs.

EGG BREAD
Southern American

½ pint white cornmeal
3 eggs, separated
⅔ cup 4% milk
⅔ cup buttermilk
¼ teaspoon salt
1 tablespoon melted lard

Preheat oven to 400 degrees.
1   Place cornmeal in bowl.
2   Beat egg yolks with the two milks mixed, add salt.
3   Beat egg whites in separate bowl until stiff peaks form.
4   Mix liquids with cornmeal until completely free of lumps. Let stand for 15 minutes.
5   Preheat a 1½- to 2-inch-deep 9-by-9-inch square pan at 400 de-grees. Pour melted lard in preheated pan, coat bottom and sides quickly.
6   Fold cornmeal mixture and egg whites, pour into pan, bake for 35 to 40 minutes or until done.

FROISE
Welsh

———

4 eggs
1 teaspoon salt
1 teaspoon baking powder
½ cup flour
1 tablespoon vegetable oil
1 tablespoon butter
dried currants
butter and powdered sugar for garnish

1 Beat eggs with fork until lemon colored and frothy.
2 Add salt and baking powder to flour, mix. Slowly mix in dry ingredients with eggs.
3 Heat oil and butter in a skillet and pour in the batter, sprinkle with the currants, tilt it in every direction, then turn over and brown other side.
4 Spread with butter and sprinkle with powdered sugar. Cut into 4 wedges and serve hot.

GOULASH AND SPAETZLE
Hungarian

———

2 pounds beef chuck, cut into 1-inch cubes

SALT MIXTURE
2 teaspoons salt
1 teaspoon sweet Hungarian paprika
½ teaspoon black pepper
pinch of garlic salt

½ cup lard or chicken fat
2½ to 3 cups onions, measured, peeled, and finely chopped

2 tablespoons sweet Hungarian paprika (optional)
2 tablespoons flour
3 cups water or beef stock
2 tablespoons tomato paste
1 teaspoon caraway seeds, slightly bruised

1   Season meat with salt mixture.
2   In large, heavy saucepan, heat lard or fat to smoking point. Quickly fry the meat, turning with a spatula so it browns evenly. Add onions, stir well, and cook until limp. Sprinkle paprika and flour over the meat and onions. Cook for 2 minutes on low heat, stirring to keep from sticking.
3   Add water or beef stock, tomato paste, and caraway seeds. Stir. Simmer covered over low heat for 1½ hours or until meat is tender. Add more liquid if necessary.
4   When ready, gravy should barely cover meat. Let it stand for 1 hour to greatly improve the taste. Serve from a large casserole. Serves 6.

Note:

Whenever available, add half a bell pepper cut into strips or a whole Hungarian pepper when you add the liquid and tomato paste.

The word *goulash*—in Hungarian *gulyas*—means "cowboy" or "herdsman," and the full name of the dish, *gulyas-hus*, means "herdsman's meat."

GALUSKA / SPAETZLE
water with salt
4 eggs
1 cup milk
3 cups flour
1 teaspoon salt
4 to 6 tablespoons butter

1   Fill a large pot about two-thirds with water. Add approximately 1 teaspoon salt for each quart of water. Cover and bring to a boil, then set heat for gentle boil.

2   With large fork, beat eggs with the milk. In a large mixing bowl, combine flour and salt with the egg mixture. Stir with a wooden spoon until the batter is smooth.

3   Dip a tablespoon into the boiling water and spoon the dough about the size of an almond into the kettle. Continue with all the dough.

4   Cover the pot, leaving an opening so steam and foam can escape. Stir occasionally. Cook until all the *galuska* are floating. Test one by cutting through it to be sure no raw center remains. Pour into a colander and immediately rinse quickly and briefly with cold water. Shake dry.

5   Place *galuska* in a skillet and distribute the butter over the top. Let it melt, then gently turn the *galuska* with spatula and keep them warm until ready to serve.

HACKAD BIFF MED LOK
Minced Beef with Onions / Swedish

---

2 pounds chopped beef (80% lean preferred)
3 teaspoons salt
½ teaspoon pepper
4 tablespoons melted butter
1 onion, peeled, sliced (1½ cups)
3 tablespoons corn oil
½ cup hot water

Preheat oven to 350 degrees.

1   Season meat with salt and pepper and form into a flat, square shape on a cutting board. Divide into 16 even units. Shape into round, 1-inch-thick patties.

2   Fry in the melted butter, about 1 minute on each side.

3   Fry the sliced onion in corn oil until golden brown and place over the meat cakes. Add about ½ cup of hot water and bake 10 minutes for medium rare, 15 minutes for medium. Serve hot.

HAMANTASCHEN
Poppy Seed Cakes / Jewish

———

½ cup black poppy seeds
¼ cup sugar
1½ cups milk
½ cup honey
½ cup white raisins, soaked in hot water for 15 minutes
¼ cup chopped nuts (walnuts, almonds, or hazelnuts)
coffee cake dough
½ cup honey

Preheat oven to 375 degrees.
1   Grind the poppy seeds only in special poppy seed grinder.
2   Add sugar. Simmer in milk for 20 minutes.
3   Add other ingredients; mix well. Simmer for 10 more minutes; cool to room temperature.
4   Roll dough into a sheet about ¼ inch thick and cut into 4-inch squares. Place tablespoon of seed mixture on each square and pinch into a three-cornered cake.
5   Brush with honey and bake about 15 minutes in medium oven.

Note:

To avoid any difficulties in obtaining the right poppy seed, prepared canned SOLO poppy seed is generally available in supermarkets and specialty food shops. A poppy seed grinder is available at Szalay Brothers European Sausage House, 4361 North Lincoln Avenue, Chicago, IL 60646 (312-472-9645).

If you cannot get a satisfactory coffee cake dough, try, as we did, a tube of Pillsbury's ready-to-bake croissant dough. It worked fine. Another quick and satisfying method was to prepare the Pillsbury's pie-dough sticks according to package directions.

HARVEST HOME DRINK
American

————

2½ gallons cold water
1 quart molasses
1 cup vinegar (Heinz white vinegar)
1 ounce ground ginger

Mix all and serve cold.

Note:

We didn't know how we would like this "American" soft drink, so we tried it. It was interesting . . . but we are members of the "Pepsi generation."

LE HOCHEPOT
Hotchpotch / Belgian

————

1 pound brisket of beef
1 pound shoulder or breast of lamb
1 pound shoulder or neck of veal
1 pound pigs' feet
½ pound pigs' tails
4 tablespoons salt
½ teaspoon pepper
cold water to cover
½ head of cabbage cut into 4 wedges
1 carrot cut into 4 pieces
2 leeks split in half (white part only)

2 stalks celery cut into 4 pieces
6 small white onions (peeled, uncut)
2 tablespoons additional salt
6 black peppercorns, 2 bay leaves, 1 clove garlic, ½ teaspoon tarragon,
3 cloves, all tied in cheesecloth bag

1   Rub all the meat strongly with salt and pepper and put into kettle. Cover with cold water and bring to boiling point over high heat. Adjust heat to medium. Skim well until scum stops rising.
2   Add the vegetables sliced and seasoned with salt.
3   Put spices in cheesecloth bag and add.
4   When all meat is tender, arrange on platter surrounded by the vegetables. The soup is served as a separate course.

LUKEFISK
Minced Fish / Norwegian

――――

5 tablespoons butter
¼ cup flour
1½ cups hot milk
salt to taste
pepper to taste
nutmeg to taste
1 cup boiled minced fish
1 cup diced boiled potatoes

1   Melt butter in saucepan.
2   Mix flour into the milk, leaving no lumps. Add mixture slowly to the hot butter and stir with a wire whip constantly until thick.
3   Season with salt, pepper, and nutmeg to taste.
4   Carefully fold in fish and potatoes and cook 5 minutes.

Note:

We tested this dish with several different fish. The plainest was codfish; we needed 1 pound. Salmon was elegant but expensive; it was very good. Monkfish was wasteful but good; Boston scrod, just so-so. White-fish was a great hit with those who don't care much for a fishy taste.

MEXICAN RICE
Mexican

———

1 cup rice
2 tablespoons butter
1 cup tomato sauce
1 teaspoon sugar
2 teaspoons salt
2 cups boiling water

1   Wash rice and dry.
2   Melt butter in frying pan and add the rice. Fry until light brown, stirring constantly.
3   Add tomato sauce, sugar, and salt; simmer 5 minutes.
4   Add boiling water, stir well, adjust heat to low, cover and cook until rice is tender.

OLLEBROD
Beer Bread / Danish

———

1-pound loaf rye bread
½ cup water
2 pint bottles or 1 quart pale ale
sugar to taste (we used ½ cup)
½ teaspoon grated lemon rind (yellow "zest" only)
1 pint cream

1   Cut crust off bread loaf. Slice, then cut into small cubes and soak in water and 1 pint ale for at least 12 hours. Keep covered in refrigerator.

2 Place in a saucepan and simmer for 20 minutes over medium heat.
3 Rub through a sieve with a wooden spoon, discard seeds, and return to saucepan.
4 Add the other pint of ale and bring to boiling point.
5 Add sugar to taste and lemon rind. Boil a few minutes longer and serve with cream.

POLENTA
Yellow Cornmeal Mush / Italian

———

1 cup yellow cornmeal
4 cups boiling water
1 teaspoon salt

1 Stir the cornmeal slowly, using a wooden spoon, into the boiling salted water over high heat. Adjust to medium and cook until mush is thick. It will take 25 to 35 minutes. Be careful, the hot mixture will start to "puff" and shoot out hot cornmeal bubbles.
2 Pour into shallow pan to cool and harden.

SAUCE FOR POLENTA
1 pound chicken liver
1 cup finely diced onion
1 tablespoon butter
1 tablespoon lard
1 teaspoon salt
1 cup water
1 tablespoon flour
black pepper and oregano to taste

1 Cut chicken liver into small cubes.
2 Brown finely diced onion in the butter and lard over high heat.
3 Add the chicken liver and sauté; season with salt. Reduce heat to medium, cook 5 minutes.

4   Mix water with the flour and thickened onion-liver mixture. Season with black pepper and oregano.

5   Pour over slices of polenta.

Note:

When we made this dish with the kidneys called for in the original recipe, it was not popular with our taste panel. But when we did it with the liver, most people liked it. And changing it to ½ pound chicken liver and ½ pound Italian sausage, removed from the casing and mixed with the liver, made it even more popular.

PROSIAK FASZEROWANY
Stuffed Suckling Pig / Polish

———

1 small suckling pig, about 16 to 22 pounds
4 to 6 tablespoons salt mixed with ½ teaspoon black and ½ teaspoon white
pepper, 1 tablespoon paprika, and ½ teaspoon garlic salt
2 pounds pure lard
1 quart beer
10½-ounce can chicken broth, undiluted
3 tablespoons flour
½ cup cold water

STUFFING
2 cups coarsely chopped onion
¾ cup butter
2 goose livers (or 8 to 10 duck livers)
½ pound mushrooms, chopped
1 tablespoon chopped parsley
½ teaspoon dry dillweed
marjoram to taste
tarragon to taste
salt and pepper to taste
2 eggs

1   Prepare cookie sheet or other pan large enough to hold the suckling pig on its stomach with hind legs pulled up under the body and head stretched out on forelegs. Brush pan with shortening, line with aluminum foil also brushed with shortening.

2   Wash and dry the pig inside and outside, rubbing the surface completely dry with towels. Rub inside with salt mixture; avoid getting any salt on outside of skin. Tie hind legs together under the belly; allow enough room between legs so belly can be stuffed and sewn. Tie front legs together.

3   Preheat oven to 375 degrees. Prepare stuffing by browning chopped onion in butter. Chop stuffing ingredients except eggs and add to the browned onion with the seasonings. Add eggs and mix well. Spoon mixture to fill the belly cavity; sew opening with white string.

4   Thickly spread lard over the entire skin, covering back especially well. Place pig in preheated oven. After 1 hour, dip towel in beer and wipe entire skin. Repeat every 15 minutes. Toward the end of the cooking time (about 3½ to 4 hours) wipe every 10 minutes.

5   Remove pig when thermometer inserted into thickest part of hind leg registers 175 to 180 degrees. When cool enough to be handled, place pig on serving platter surrounded with parsley or other greens.

6   Serve with sauce made by scraping all the beer and fat mixture from the foil-lined pan and diluting it with chicken broth. Then thicken with flour dissolved in cold water.
Serves 8 to 12.

Note:

Use government-inspected suckling pig.

To carve, first cut off the head by inserting sharp knife about 1½ to 2 inches below the ears, toward center of a joint between the neck bones. Split pig on either side of backbone, cutting from neck to tail. On one half, cut off whole hind leg, then front leg, using shorter-bladed knife. Now cut the rib into serving-size pieces. Slice or cut up the legs. Repeat with other half of pig. Spoon stuffing on a platter for guests to help themselves.

PUDIM DE NOSES
Walnut Pudding / Portuguese

———

½ pound walnuts (1 full cup)
4 large eggs, separated
1 cup sugar
½ teaspoon cinnamon
pinch of salt

Preheat oven to 350 degrees.

1   Grind walnuts in a food processor until completely mashed.

2   Bring water to boil in large pan to accommodate oven-proof pudding mold. Brush mold with melted butter.

3   Beat egg yolks at high speed with electric mixer with 1 tablespoon sugar until lemony and frothy. Slowly add rest of sugar and cinnamon. Keep at high speed until well mixed. Remove from mixer and fold walnuts in slowly with a rubber spatula. Scrape bottom.

4   In a second mixing bowl, add 2 egg whites with a pinch of salt. Beat until firm peaks form. Add other 2 egg whites, re-whip. It will first collapse but re-form into firmer peaks. Fold half of whites into egg yolks–nut mixture until completely mixed. Fold in second half, distribute whites evenly. Transfer mixture to pudding mold. Cover with lid or foil. Submerge in pot of boiling water. Place in pre-heated oven and bake 45 minutes or until firm. Can be served hot or cold, with whipped cream or a fine Portuguese dessert wine. Serves 8.

SEED CAKE
Welsh

———

½ cake yeast (1 ounce)
½ cup lukewarm water
1 cup sugar
2 cups flour

½ cup shortening (we used butter)
1 teaspoon salt
1 teaspoon caraway seeds
2 eggs

Preheat oven to 375 degrees.
1   Dissolve yeast in lukewarm water, add 1 teaspoon sugar, 1 table-spoon flour. Let rise.
2   Cream butter with rest of sugar. When fluffy, add alternately rest of flour mixed with other dry ingredients and well-beaten eggs. End with flour.
3   When mixed well, place in a buttered cake mold.
4   Let rise to double size and bake about 1 hour.

SOUPA AVGHOLEMONO
Lemon Soup / Greek

———

1 tablespoon rice
1 quart chicken soup or 1 quart water and
1 tablespoon Minor's chicken base
2 egg yolks
2 tablespoons warm water
3 tablespoons lemon juice

1   Boil rice in the chicken soup until tender.
2   Mix yolks with warm water and stir into soup with lemon juice.
3   Serve as soon as ready.

SPAGHETTI SAUCE
Italian

———

1 cup minced onion
1 clove of garlic, peeled
¼ cup olive oil

1 6-ounce can tomato paste
1½ cups water
½ cup chopped green pepper
½ cup chopped red pepper
1 heaping tablespoon sugar
pinch of oregano
boiled spaghetti

1   Mince onion, add garlic, and cook slowly in oil. Onion should be cooked thoroughly but not browned. Remove and discard garlic.
2   Add tomato paste, ½ cup water, and green and red peppers cut in tiny pieces. Add sugar and oregano; cook 5 more minutes.
3   Add the rest of the water and cook covered for 1 hour over low heat.
4   Serve with boiled spaghetti.

STOKVISCH
Stock Fish / Dutch

———

1 pound dried codfish
salt
baked onions
rice
mustard sauce

1   Soak the cod in cold water for 12 hours.
2   Skin, bone, and slice into 6 long strips. Roll each slice and tie with strong string.
3   Simmer in salted water for 1 hour.
4   Remove string and serve with baked onions, rice, and mustard sauce.

Note:

When you shop for dried codfish, you may be surprised how many ethnic groups rely on it as a staple. Portuguese, Spanish, Scandinavian, and Oriental stores all sell it. Be sure you give yourself enough time for preparation after the 12 hours of soaking.

TADJIN AHMAR
Mutton Stew with Prunes / Arabian

———

4 pounds lamb neck or shoulder, cut into 2-inch strips
1½ tablespoons salt
½ cup olive oil
1 cup finely minced onion
boiling water to cover the meat
1 stick cinnamon 2½ to 3 inches long
pinch of saffron softened in a little hot water (optional)
1 pound pitted California prunes
2 tablespoons sugar or to taste

Preheat oven to 350 degrees.
1 Cut lamb into 2-inch strips and season with salt.
2 Brown meat in olive oil. Place in casserole and add minced onion, boiling water, cinnamon, and softened saffron. Mix and bake about ½ hour in preheated oven.
3 Add prunes and sugar and bake another ½ hour.
4 Serve in casserole.

TIN SUIN PAI KWE
Pork with Sweet-Sour Sauce / Chinese

———

SWEET-SOUR SAUCE
pinch of salt
2 cloves garlic
1 ounce Chinese or Japanese vinegar

2 cups water

¼ cup sugar

2 teaspoons soy sauce

3 tablespoons cornstarch mixed with ½ cup water

¼ teaspoon black pepper

½ cup pineapple chunks

1 cup each red and green pepper cut into ½ inch squares

1 cup onions cut into ½ inch squares

1 cup cut sweet gherkins (optional)

PORK

1 pound boneless pork cutlets, cut into approximately 2-by-2-inch pieces

salt and pepper to taste

¼ cup flour

2 eggs

oil for frying

1 tablespoon sesame oil

1   Prepare sweet-sour sauce first. Sprinkle a little salt into oiled frying pan.
2   Crush the garlic cloves and cook for a few seconds. Remove garlic, add vinegar, water, sugar, soy sauce, cornstarch mixture, and black pepper. Add pineapple, red and green peppers, onions, and gherkins if desired. Keep simmering on low heat.
3   Season meat with salt and pepper and coat with flour.
4   Beat eggs and dip the meat in.
5   Cook meat in hot oil in 2 or 3 batches for 10 minutes each. Remove from the oil and drain on paper towel.
6   Place meat in sauce, add sesame oil, stir for about 2 minutes, and serve with hot rice.

Note:

You may add a few drops of red food coloring into 1 tablespoon of the sauce, then add it to the rest.

WIENER SCHNITZEL
Vienna Veal Steak / Austrian

———

4 thin slices veal (approximately 4 ounces each from the leg or
5 to 6 ounces "bone in" from the loin)
salt and pepper
2 tablespoons flour
1 egg mixed with 1 tablespoon water
2 cups white bread crumbs
6 to 8 tablespoons fat (half butter, half lard or oil)
lemon wedges for garnish

Preheat oven to 250 degrees.

1   Sprinkle veal with salt and pepper.
2   Dip each slice in flour, then in well-beaten egg, then in bread crumbs.
3   Heat fat and fry schnitzels until light brown. Turn once.
4   Finish baking in preheated oven about 20 minutes.
5   Serve with lemon.

Note:

This dish is traditionally served with mashed or home-fried potatoes or German potato salad and a green salad of lettuce with light vinaigrette.

ZABAGLIONE
Italian

———

3 egg yolks
1½ tablespoons sugar
just over ½ cup sherry
1 teaspoon lemon juice